Quantum Cashflow

Quantum Cashflow

Matthew Petchinsky

1

Quantum Cashflow: The 10-Minute Formula for Infinite Wealth

By: Matthew Petchinsky

Disclaimer

Quantum Cashflow: The 10-Minute Formula for Infinite Wealth is intended solely for educational, informational, and personal development purposes. The ideas, strategies, examples, and exercises presented throughout this book are designed to encourage readers to think critically about money, productivity, opportunity, financial decision-making, and long-term wealth creation. Nothing contained within this book should be interpreted as financial, investment, legal, accounting, tax, medical, or other professional advice.

The title and concepts presented in this book use the terms *quantum* and *infinite wealth* as metaphors for expanded thinking, continuous learning, innovation, opportunity recognition, and the potential for long-term financial growth. They are not intended to imply scientifically proven methods for generating wealth, supernatural abilities, guaranteed financial outcomes, or limitless monetary returns. Readers should understand these concepts as motivational and conceptual frameworks rather than literal claims.

Every individual's financial circumstances are unique. Income, expenses, debt, investments, employment opportunities, education, market conditions, geographic location, health, experience, and countless other factors influence financial outcomes. As a result, no strategy, habit, system, or framework can guarantee financial success. Any examples, illustrations, projections, or case studies included in this book are provided solely to demonstrate concepts and should not be interpreted as promises of future performance.

The author and publisher make no representations, warranties, or guarantees regarding any specific financial result, investment return, business success, income level, asset accumulation, debt reduction, or wealth achieved through the use of the information presented in this book. Readers accept full responsibility for evaluating, adapting, and implementing any ideas according to their own circumstances and risk tolerance.

Whenever financial decisions involve significant sums of money, legal obligations, taxation, retirement planning, investments, insurance, business formation, lending, real estate, cryptocurrency, securities, or other regulated financial activities, readers are strongly encouraged to consult appropriately qualified professionals before taking action. Professional guidance should always take precedence over general educational material.

The exercises contained throughout this book are intended to encourage reflection, planning, organization, and personal accountability. Completing these exercises does not guarantee financial improvement, increased income, successful investments, or business profitability. Their effectiveness depends upon consistent application, informed decision-making, ongoing education, discipline, changing economic conditions, and many external variables beyond anyone's control.

Markets change. Technologies evolve. Economic conditions fluctuate. Laws, regulations, tax policies, and financial products are continually updated. Information that is accurate at the time of publication may change over time. Readers should verify current information through reliable and authoritative sources before making important financial decisions.

Any references to businesses, industries, investment vehicles, financial concepts, technologies, or economic trends are provided solely for educational discussion. Such references do not constitute endorsements, recommendations, or solicitations to buy, sell, invest, or participate in any specific financial product, company, or opportunity.

The author encourages readers to pursue ethical, lawful, and responsible methods of wealth creation. Sustainable prosperity is best built through integrity, education, continuous improvement, thoughtful planning, disciplined execution, prudent risk management, and respect for applicable laws and regulations.

By reading this book, the reader acknowledges that all financial decisions remain their own responsibility. The author and publisher shall not be held liable for any direct, indirect, incidental, consequential, financial, legal, or other damages arising from the use or misuse of the information contained within this publication.

May this book serve as a source of inspiration, practical thinking, and disciplined action as you develop your own path toward greater financial knowledge, opportunity, resilience, and long-term prosperity.

Introduction: The Quantum Shift in Wealth—How Money Is Created in Seconds

For generations, people have been taught that wealth follows a predictable path. Work hard. Save diligently. Invest patiently. Wait decades. Hope nothing unexpected happens along the way.

While there is wisdom in patience and discipline, the world has changed.

Today, fortunes can begin with a single idea shared online. A digital product can be purchased thousands of times while its creator sleeps. A software application can reach millions of users across continents within months. An investor can execute trades from a phone. An entrepreneur can launch an international business without renting an office or hiring a large staff. Artificial intelligence can complete tasks that once required entire departments. Knowledge itself has become one of the world's most valuable assets.

Money no longer moves only through factories, storefronts, or corporate boardrooms.

It moves through information.

It moves through attention.

It moves through innovation.

It moves through value.

Most importantly, it moves through decisions.

Every second, somewhere on Earth, someone purchases a book, subscribes to a service, downloads an application, invests in a company, licenses an invention, books a vacation, commissions artwork, pays a freelancer, or starts a business. Wealth is constantly being exchanged, transferred, invested, created, and multiplied through billions of individual decisions.

This realization changes everything.

The greatest financial barrier for many people is not opportunity—it is perspective.

Many people unconsciously believe wealth is scarce. They imagine there is only so much money available, that success belongs only to the lucky, the highly educated, or those born into privilege. They view financial success as something controlled by circumstances beyond their influence.

Yet every day, entirely new businesses appear.

New authors publish books.

New inventors receive patents.

New educators launch courses.

New artists build audiences.

New programmers create software.

New consultants solve problems.

New investors discover opportunities.

New entrepreneurs find underserved markets.

None of these individuals created money from nothing. They created value that others voluntarily exchanged money to receive.

That distinction is one of the central ideas of this book.

Money follows value.

Always.

When value increases, opportunities often increase alongside it.

When problems are solved, markets respond.

When people are helped, businesses grow.

When trust is established, relationships become profitable over time.

The purpose of this book is not to convince you that wealth appears through wishful thinking or magical shortcuts. Instead, it is to demonstrate how modern economies allow value to be created, shared, and exchanged at unprecedented speed.

The "quantum" in **Quantum Cashflow** is a metaphor for transformation—a dramatic shift in perspective. Just as quantum physics revealed that reality behaves differently at incredibly small scales, today's digital economy behaves differently than the financial systems many people were taught to navigate.

Distance matters less.

Time matters less.

Gatekeepers matter less.

Ideas matter more.

Creativity matters more.

Adaptability matters more.

Knowledge matters more.

The speed at which value can move from one person to millions has fundamentally changed the landscape of wealth creation.

Think about how quickly information spreads today. A useful tutorial reaches thousands of viewers in hours. A compelling article is shared across continents in minutes. A well-designed product can generate orders moments after it becomes available. A software update reaches millions of devices almost instantly. A recommendation posted online influences purchasing decisions worldwide before the day ends.

The exchange of value has accelerated.

And when value moves faster, so can cash flow.

This does not eliminate the need for hard work. In fact, it often demands greater preparation. Successful entrepreneurs spend years refining ideas before anyone notices them. Authors write hundreds of pages before publishing. Investors devote countless hours to research. Inventors repeatedly improve prototypes before introducing them to the market.

What has changed is not the importance of effort.

What has changed is the speed at which prepared effort can be rewarded.

One meaningful solution can create opportunities that continue generating income long after the original work is complete.

One exceptional book can educate readers for decades.

One useful application can serve millions.

One innovative system can save organizations countless hours.

One invention can reshape an entire industry.

One investment made after careful research can appreciate over many years.

The modern economy rewards scalable value.

Throughout this book, you will discover a practical framework built around brief, focused daily sessions. The "10-Minute Formula" is based on a simple principle: consistent, intentional action compounds over time. Ten minutes devoted each day to learning, planning, refining an idea, improving a product, studying markets, reviewing finances, or strengthening a valuable skill may seem modest in isolation. Yet those minutes accumulate into hours, weeks, months, and years of meaningful progress.

Small improvements repeated consistently often produce remarkable long-term results.

Financial transformation rarely happens because of one dramatic event. More often, it emerges from thousands of thoughtful decisions made over time. Choosing to learn instead of scroll. Choosing to budget instead of guess. Choosing to build instead of postpone. Choosing to solve problems instead of merely noticing them. Choosing to invest in knowledge that expands your ability to create value.

Each decision may take only moments.

Its consequences may last for years.

As you move through the chapters ahead, you will examine timeless principles through the lens of today's rapidly evolving economy. You will explore habits that encourage financial clarity, methods for recognizing opportunity, strategies for developing valuable skills, approaches to managing risk responsibly, and ways to build systems that can generate income beyond the hours you personally work.

None of these ideas promise effortless wealth.

They do promise something far more valuable: a mindset centered on continuous learning, disciplined action, adaptability, ethical value creation, and long-term thinking.

The world's economy is constantly evolving. New technologies will emerge. New industries will rise. Consumer needs will change. Markets will expand and contract. The individuals who thrive are rarely those who predict every change perfectly—they are the ones who remain curious, prepared, and willing to adapt.

That is the true quantum shift.

It begins not in your bank account, but in your thinking.

Because wealth is rarely created in a single extraordinary moment.

It is built through countless ordinary moments in which you choose to learn, create, improve, and serve.

Those moments may last only seconds.

Their impact can endure for a lifetime.

Welcome to **Quantum Cashflow**.

Your next decision begins now.

Chapter 1: The Quantum Wealth Principle—Why Time Is the Only Currency That Matters

----

The Value Hidden Inside Every Minute

Most people spend their lives chasing money while overlooking the one resource that makes money possible in the first place: time. From childhood onward, society conditions us to think in terms of dollars, salaries, investments, and possessions. We compare incomes, celebrate promotions, and admire expensive lifestyles, often believing that financial success is measured solely by the number printed in a bank account. Yet beneath every paycheck, every business, every invention, and every fortune lies an invisible investment that cannot be replaced once it has been spent. That investment is time. Unlike money, time cannot be borrowed indefinitely, recreated, manufactured, or earned back after it has passed. Every successful entrepreneur, investor, artist, scientist, and innovator receives exactly the same twenty-four hours each day. The difference is rarely found in how much time they possess, but rather in how intentionally they choose to use it. **Time is the foundation upon which every form of wealth is built.**

Imagine receiving $86,400 every morning with only one condition: any amount you fail to spend before midnight disappears forever. Most people would carefully consider how to use every dollar. They would invest wisely, eliminate waste, and avoid frivolous purchases. Yet every day, each of us receives something even more valuable—86,400 seconds. Unlike money, these seconds cannot be saved for tomorrow, deposited into an account, or recovered after they disappear. Once a second has passed, it becomes part of history. This simple realization transforms the way we view productivity. Financial success begins long before money enters a checking account. It begins with recognizing that every decision about how to spend one's time is also a decision about one's future opportunities. Every minute invested in learning, building, planning, practicing, or improving has the potential to produce returns that extend far beyond the original investment.

Many people mistakenly believe wealth begins with having capital. In reality, nearly every fortune begins with attention. Before there is a profitable business, someone dedicates time to solving a problem. Before there is a bestselling book, an author spends months or years writing page after page. Before a groundbreaking invention changes the world, an inventor devotes countless hours to experimentation, failure, revision, and improvement. Even inherited wealth requires time to preserve, manage, and grow responsibly. The common denominator is not money—it is focused effort over time. This is encouraging because it means that while people begin life with different financial circumstances, everyone possesses the ability to choose how today's hours influence tomorrow's possibilities.

The modern economy has made time more valuable than at any other point in history. Technology allows a single hour of thoughtful work to reach millions of people almost instantly. A digital course created over several weeks may educate students for years. A software application developed over months can generate revenue around the clock. A book written during consistent daily writing sessions can continue earning income long after publication. A useful invention can improve lives across generations. These examples demonstrate an important truth: **well-invested time can eventually work on your behalf long after the original effort has ended.** The goal is not merely to exchange hours for income but to use time creating assets that continue producing value.

This principle also explains why many people remain financially stagnant despite working extremely hard. Hard work alone does not guarantee prosperity if every hour is consumed maintaining the present without building the future. Someone may labor tirelessly each day yet devote no time to developing new skills, exploring additional income sources, improving financial literacy, or creating scalable value. In contrast, another individual may reserve just ten focused minutes every day to learn, write, design, research, invest wisely, or build a side business. Over weeks and years, those seemingly insignificant moments accumulate into extraordinary progress. **Consistency often outperforms intensity when sustained over long periods.**

Understanding time as your primary currency also changes how you evaluate opportunities. Instead of asking, "How much money will this make?" you begin asking, **"Is this the highest and best use of my time?"** Some activities produce immediate income but no future growth. Others require patience but build knowledge, relationships, systems, or assets that continue creating value for years. Learning to distinguish between spending time and investing time is one of the defining characteristics of financially successful people. Every hour should be viewed as a seed. Some seeds produce quick harvests, while others grow into forests that provide abundance for generations.

One of the greatest misconceptions about wealth is that it arrives through one extraordinary breakthrough. While breakthrough moments certainly exist, they are usually supported by hundreds or thousands of ordinary days spent learning, refining skills, making mistakes, improving systems, and remaining committed despite slow progress. Wealth is often the visible result of invisible habits repeated consistently over time. The person who writes one page each day eventually completes a book. The investor who studies markets regularly develops greater confidence. The entrepreneur who improves one aspect of a business every day gradually builds a stronger enterprise. **Small investments of time create compound results that are often invisible until they become impossible to ignore.**

As you begin this journey through *Quantum Cashflow*, remember this foundational principle: **money is renewable, but time is not.** A financial loss can often be recovered through learning, perseverance, and disciplined action. A missed opportunity may lead to another opportunity in the future. However, yesterday's hours can never be reclaimed. Every new day presents a fresh allocation of the world's most valuable resource. How you choose to invest those hours will shape your knowledge, your habits, your opportunities, your relationships, your financial future, and ultimately the legacy you leave behind. Before mastering money, you must first learn to master time. It is the first investment every wealthy life is built upon.

From Trading Hours to Creating Value

One of the greatest financial lessons a person can learn is that there is a significant difference between earning money and creating value. Most people begin their financial journey by exchanging time directly for income. They work an hour and receive an agreed-upon wage. This arrangement is neither good nor bad—it is simply the starting point for many careers. However, those who achieve lasting financial independence eventually discover that wealth grows most effectively when value becomes disconnected from the number of hours worked. **The goal is not merely to work harder than everyone else but to create something that continues benefiting others long after the original work has been completed.**

Consider a carpenter who builds a custom dining table. The carpenter invests knowledge, craftsmanship, creativity, and labor into producing something another person values enough to purchase. The buyer is not paying solely for the hours involved. They are paying for years of experience, attention to detail, problem-solving ability, artistic judgment, and dependable quality. Likewise, an author is not compensated simply for the hours spent writing but for the knowledge, entertainment, education, or inspiration the finished book provides to readers. A software developer creates tools that save businesses countless hours, while an engineer designs systems that improve efficiency for entire industries. **In every case, money follows value rather than effort alone.**

This principle explains why two people can work equally hard yet experience vastly different financial outcomes. One individual may perform repetitive tasks that generate value only while actively working. Another may spend time developing a skill, creating an asset, or building a system that serves thousands or even millions of people. Neither person's effort should be dismissed, but the scalability of the value they create is very different. A single well-designed online course, useful mobile application, licensing agreement, invention, or published book can continue helping people repeatedly without requiring the creator to repeat every hour of labor for every customer.

The modern economy has dramatically expanded the opportunities to create scalable value. Digital technology allows knowledge, creativity, and innovation to travel farther and faster than ever before. A musician can distribute songs worldwide in minutes. An educator can teach students across continents without leaving home. A designer can sell templates to customers in dozens of countries. An entrepreneur can launch a business with relatively modest startup costs compared to previous generations. These developments do not eliminate competition, but they do reduce many of the traditional barriers that once limited opportunity. **Today, one well-executed idea has the potential to reach an audience that earlier generations could scarcely imagine.**

Creating value also requires developing the habit of solving problems. Every successful product or service exists because it answers a question, removes frustration, saves time, improves comfort, reduces cost, increases efficiency, provides enjoyment, or fulfills a meaningful need. Businesses rarely succeed because they simply exist; they succeed because they make life better in some measurable way. The greater the problem solved, the more valuable the solution often becomes. Instead of constantly asking, "How can I make more money?" begin asking, **"What problem can I solve exceptionally well?"** That single shift in thinking can reshape an entire financial future.

Value is not limited to products or businesses. It also exists in personal character. Reliability creates value. Honesty creates value. Clear communication creates value. Leadership creates value. Kindness, professionalism, consistency, and trustworthiness all contribute to opportunities that may not produce immediate financial rewards but often generate long-term relationships and reputations that are invaluable. Employers, clients, partners, and customers naturally gravitate toward people they trust. Reputation becomes a form of invisible capital that grows stronger each time promises are kept and excellence becomes a habit.

An important part of the Quantum Wealth Principle is recognizing that every day offers an opportunity to increase your personal value.

Reading one chapter of a useful book, learning a new software skill, practicing public speaking, improving financial literacy, studying marketing, refining writing ability, strengthening leadership, or understanding customer psychology may not immediately increase your income tomorrow morning. Yet each improvement expands your capacity to contribute something meaningful. Over time, these seemingly modest investments compound into expertise that becomes increasingly valuable in the marketplace. **The person you become ultimately determines the value you are capable of creating.**

As you continue through this book, remember that lasting wealth is rarely the result of chasing money directly. Instead, it emerges from consistently increasing the value you bring into the lives of others. Every new skill mastered, every problem solved, every relationship strengthened, every lesson learned, and every asset created expands your ability to contribute to the world. When value becomes your primary focus, money often follows as a natural consequence of the positive impact you create. **Your greatest financial asset is not found in your wallet, your investment account, or your business—it is your continually growing ability to create value that improves the lives of others.**

The Compounding Power of Ten Focused Minutes

One of the most overlooked principles of wealth creation is that extraordinary results rarely require extraordinary beginnings. Many people postpone pursuing financial goals because they believe they need several uninterrupted hours each day, a large amount of startup capital, or perfect conditions before they can make meaningful progress. This belief often leads to procrastination disguised as preparation. The truth is far simpler and far more empowering: **small, consistent actions performed every day frequently produce greater long-term results than occasional bursts of intense effort.** The purpose of the 10-Minute Formula is to demonstrate that focused consistency can become one of the most valuable financial habits you ever develop.

Ten minutes may seem insignificant when viewed in isolation. After all, ten minutes passes quickly. It can disappear while scrolling through social media, watching television, checking unnecessary notifications, or worrying about problems without taking action. Yet when those same ten minutes are invested intentionally, they begin accumulating into something remarkably powerful. Ten focused minutes every day becomes over an hour each week, dozens of hours each year, and hundreds of hours over several years. Those accumulated hours represent time spent acquiring knowledge, developing skills, building assets, refining ideas, strengthening relationships, or improving financial systems. **Consistency quietly transforms small moments into substantial achievements.**

Think about the way compound interest works in finance. At first, growth appears slow because the gains are relatively small. Over time, however, those gains begin generating additional gains, creating an accelerating cycle of growth. Personal development operates in much the same way. Learning one new financial concept each day expands your understanding. That understanding improves future decisions. Better decisions lead to improved habits. Improved habits create stronger opportunities. Those opportunities often generate greater confidence, which encourages even more learning and action. Before long, what began as ten minutes of focused effort becomes the foundation for significant personal and financial growth. **Compounding is not limited to money—it also applies to knowledge, discipline, confidence, and opportunity.**

Many successful people have one characteristic in common: they make productive use of small pockets of time that others overlook. They read while waiting for appointments, outline business ideas during lunch breaks, review investments before work, listen to educational material while commuting, or spend a few focused minutes each evening improving an important project. They understand that progress does not always require dramatic life changes. Instead, it often requires protecting brief periods of uninterrupted concentration. These moments may seem ordinary, but over months and years they produce extraordinary outcomes because they are repeated consistently without interruption.

The effectiveness of ten focused minutes depends entirely on the quality of attention invested during those minutes. A distracted hour often accomplishes less than ten minutes of concentrated effort. During focused work, distractions are minimized, objectives are clearly defined, and energy is directed toward one meaningful task. This practice strengthens not only productivity but also the ability to concentrate for longer periods in the future. Like any skill, focus improves with repetition. The more consistently you train your attention, the easier it becomes to accomplish meaningful work efficiently. **Your ability to focus is one of the most valuable economic skills you can develop in an increasingly distracted world.**

The 10-Minute Formula can be applied to nearly every area of wealth creation. You might dedicate ten minutes each morning to studying investing principles, reviewing a household budget, brainstorming business ideas, writing a page of a future book, researching market trends, improving marketing skills, learning artificial intelligence tools, strengthening negotiation techniques, or reaching out to potential clients and collaborators. Each activity contributes to increasing your knowledge and expanding your opportunities. None of these actions may seem life-changing on a single day, but together they create momentum that becomes difficult to stop.

Equally important is recognizing that momentum often matters more than speed. Many people abandon worthwhile goals because they compare their beginning to someone else's years of experience. This comparison creates discouragement and often leads to quitting before meaningful progress becomes visible. The individual who remains committed to daily improvement, however, steadily builds confidence through action. Every completed session reinforces the identity of someone who follows through on commitments. Over time, this identity becomes stronger than temporary emotions or occasional setbacks. **Success is often less about motivation and more about maintaining forward momentum, even when progress appears slow.**

As you continue reading this book, remember that financial transformation is seldom the result of one perfect decision. More often, it is the cumulative effect of hundreds of small, intelligent decisions made consistently over time. The ten minutes you invest today may introduce an idea that changes your career tomorrow. A single page written today may become part of a bestselling book years from now. One conversation may lead to a lifelong partnership. One lesson may prevent an expensive mistake. Never underestimate the power of seemingly modest actions repeated faithfully. **The path to lasting wealth is rarely built in giant leaps—it is built one focused minute, one disciplined habit, and one intentional decision at a time.**

Choosing Investments That Multiply Your Time

One of the defining characteristics of financially successful individuals is that they learn to distinguish between activities that consume time and activities that multiply time. Every person has the same twenty-four hours each day, yet some individuals seem capable of accomplishing far more than others. The difference is not that they possess additional hours; it is that they deliberately invest their time into systems, skills, relationships, and assets that continue producing value long after the initial effort has been completed. **The wealthiest resource you can build is not more hours—it is leverage.** Leverage allows a single investment of time to generate benefits repeatedly, freeing you to pursue even greater opportunities.

Time multiplication begins with education. Every new skill you master has the potential to save countless hours in the future. Learning keyboard shortcuts, financial literacy, project management, marketing, negotiation, communication, or emerging technologies may require focused effort today, but those skills reduce mistakes, improve efficiency, and increase effectiveness for years to come. Consider the difference between someone who spends an hour struggling with unfamiliar software and someone who invested several days mastering it months earlier. The expert completes the task faster, produces higher-quality results, and has additional time available for other productive work. **Knowledge is one of the few investments that can continue paying dividends throughout an entire lifetime.**

Another powerful way to multiply time is by creating systems instead of repeatedly solving the same problems. A system is simply a reliable process that allows tasks to be completed consistently and efficiently. Businesses use systems to manage operations, authors use writing schedules to maintain momentum, investors follow predefined strategies to reduce emotional decision-making, and households rely on budgets and routines to simplify financial management. Every system removes unnecessary decision fatigue, allowing more mental energy to be directed toward meaningful opportunities. Rather than asking yourself every day what you should do next, well-designed systems answer that question automatically.

Technology has become one of the greatest time multipliers in human history when used intentionally. Automation can handle repetitive administrative tasks, organize information, schedule appointments, process transactions, and assist with research. Artificial intelligence can accelerate brainstorming, editing, organization, data analysis, and creative workflows while leaving final judgment and decision-making in human hands. Digital platforms allow creators to distribute books, courses, software, artwork, and educational content around the world without requiring physical storefronts. Used wisely, technology enables individuals to serve more people while investing less time in repetitive processes. **Technology should serve your goals rather than consume your attention.**

Relationships also function as powerful multipliers of time and opportunity. No one achieves lasting success entirely alone. Mentors shorten learning curves by sharing hard-earned experience. Business partners contribute complementary strengths. Professional networks introduce opportunities that might otherwise remain invisible. Trusted advisors help identify costly mistakes before they occur. Supportive communities encourage accountability during difficult seasons. Building genuine relationships requires patience and integrity, but over time those connections become invaluable sources of wisdom, collaboration, encouragement, and opportunity. **Your network is not merely a collection of contacts—it is a community of shared knowledge and mutual growth.**

Assets provide another remarkable example of time multiplication. Unlike wages, which generally require continuous effort to generate income, assets have the potential to continue producing value after they have been created or acquired. A published book may educate readers and generate royalties for years. A carefully developed online course may continue serving students around the world. Dividend-paying investments, rental properties, licensed intellectual property, software applications, and other productive assets can create ongoing cash flow when managed responsibly. Building assets often demands considerable patience and discipline at the beginning, but their long-term value lies in their ability to continue working even when you are focused elsewhere. **Assets transform today's effort into tomorrow's opportunity.**

Not every investment of time produces equal returns, which is why intentional evaluation is essential. Before committing your energy to a project, habit, or opportunity, ask yourself whether it contributes to long-term growth or merely fills the day with activity. Some tasks are necessary but temporary. Others create knowledge, relationships, systems, or assets that continue delivering benefits far into the future. Learning to recognize this distinction enables you to prioritize activities with the greatest lasting impact. The goal is not to remain busy but to remain productive in ways that steadily increase your capacity to create value.

As you embrace the Quantum Wealth Principle, begin viewing every hour as an investment rather than an expense. Each decision either strengthens or weakens your future opportunities. Every book you read expands your perspective. Every skill you develop increases your value. Every meaningful relationship broadens your possibilities. Every system you build improves your efficiency. Every asset you create has the potential to generate benefits beyond the time originally invested. **When you consistently choose investments that multiply your time instead of merely consuming it, you begin building a financial future that grows stronger with each passing day.**

Living Like Time Is Your Greatest Asset

Every financial decision begins long before money changes hands. It begins with a choice about how you will spend the next hour, the next afternoon, or the next week. People often believe that wealth is created in banks, stock markets, boardrooms, or business deals. While those places certainly play important roles, the true birthplace of wealth is much quieter. It is found in the daily decisions made when no one is watching—the decision to read instead of mindlessly scrolling, to practice instead of procrastinate, to learn instead of complain, and to build instead of merely consume. **Your future financial life is quietly shaped by the way you choose to spend today's time.**

Living as though time is your greatest asset requires adopting a long-term perspective. Modern culture frequently encourages instant gratification. Advertisements promise overnight success, social media showcases seemingly effortless achievements, and headlines often celebrate rapid wealth without revealing the years of preparation behind it. This constant exposure can create unrealistic expectations, causing people to underestimate the importance of steady progress. Yet history consistently demonstrates that enduring wealth is more often the product of patience than speed. Great companies, respected careers, valuable intellectual property, successful investment portfolios, and trusted reputations are typically built through years of disciplined effort. **The most powerful financial strategy is often the willingness to think farther into the future than the average person.**

One practical way to honor your time is by conducting regular personal audits. At the end of each day or week, ask yourself where your hours actually went. Which activities moved you closer to your goals? Which ones simply filled time without creating lasting value? Honest reflection is not about guilt or self-criticism; it is about awareness. Many people are surprised to discover how much time quietly disappears through distractions, unnecessary interruptions, indecision, or habits that provide temporary entertainment but little lasting benefit. Awareness creates the opportunity for improvement. **You cannot effectively manage what you do not intentionally measure.**

Living with purpose also means learning to say no. Every commitment carries an invisible cost because accepting one opportunity often means declining another. Time spent on low-value activities cannot simultaneously be invested in learning a skill, strengthening relationships, improving health, or building financial assets. Successful individuals are rarely defined only by the opportunities they accept. They are equally defined by the distractions they politely decline. Protecting your calendar is one of the most practical ways to protect your future. Every thoughtful "no" creates space for a more meaningful "yes."

Equally important is recognizing that protecting time does not mean eliminating rest. Rest is not the opposite of productivity—it is one of its essential foundations. Physical health, mental clarity, emotional resilience, creativity, and sound decision-making all depend upon adequate sleep, balanced routines, healthy relationships, and moments of genuine renewal. Constant exhaustion often leads to poor financial choices, reduced concentration, missed opportunities, and avoidable mistakes. Sustainable success requires both focused work and intentional recovery. **Your ability to create value tomorrow depends greatly on how well you care for yourself today.**

Living as though time is your greatest asset also transforms the way you approach learning. Instead of viewing education as something that ends after formal schooling, you begin treating it as a lifelong investment. Every book, podcast, lecture, workshop, conversation, and meaningful experience expands your understanding of the world. Markets evolve. Technologies advance. Industries transform. New opportunities continually emerge. Those who remain curious position themselves to recognize possibilities that others overlook. Continuous learning is not merely an academic exercise—it is one of the strongest forms of financial preparation available.

Another hallmark of people who value their time is intentional action. They understand that perfect conditions rarely exist. Waiting until every uncertainty disappears often results in missed opportunities. Instead, they gather reliable information, make thoughtful decisions, begin with manageable steps, and improve through experience. Progress creates confidence, while inaction often strengthens fear. Every completed task, every lesson learned, every skill practiced, and every problem solved contributes to a stronger foundation for future success. **Action, supported by wisdom and preparation, consistently outperforms endless hesitation.**

As you conclude this chapter, remember the central lesson of the Quantum Wealth Principle: **time is the first investment from which all other forms of wealth are born.** Money may increase and decrease throughout life. Markets will rise and fall. Careers will evolve. Technologies will change. Opportunities will appear in unexpected places. Yet every achievement will trace its origins back to moments when someone chose to invest time with intention rather than spend it carelessly. Begin treating every day as an opportunity to invest in your future self. Protect your hours, develop your abilities, strengthen your character, create lasting value, and remain faithful to the small daily decisions that compound into extraordinary results. When you learn to value your time above everything else, you build a foundation upon which lasting wealth, meaningful success, and enduring fulfillment can confidently stand.

The Quantum Wealth Mindset

Every remarkable financial journey begins with a shift in thinking long before it appears in a bank account. Wealth is not simply a collection of possessions or investments; it is the product of habits, beliefs, decisions, and actions repeated over time. Two people may begin with similar resources yet experience dramatically different outcomes because they interpret opportunities differently. One person sees obstacles and limitations, while another sees lessons and possibilities. **Your financial future is shaped first by your mindset, then by your actions, and finally by your results.**

A quantum wealth mindset recognizes that every day presents countless opportunities to create value. Rather than waiting for the perfect job, the perfect investment, or the perfect economic climate, individuals with this perspective ask themselves, *"What can I improve today?"* They understand that meaningful progress often comes from solving one problem, learning one new skill, strengthening one relationship, or completing one important task. These seemingly modest improvements accumulate over months and years into significant financial and personal growth. **Small decisions, consistently repeated, often produce extraordinary outcomes.**

Another characteristic of the quantum wealth mindset is personal responsibility. This does not mean blaming oneself for every challenge or pretending that external circumstances do not matter. Economic conditions, health, unexpected setbacks, and life events all influence financial opportunities. However, while people cannot control every circumstance, they can control how they respond. They can choose to continue learning, adapt to changing conditions, seek creative solutions, and maintain disciplined financial habits. This focus on controllable actions creates resilience, one of the greatest advantages in any economy. **Lasting wealth belongs not to those who never face adversity but to those who continue growing through it.**

People with a quantum wealth mindset also understand that mistakes are valuable teachers. Every entrepreneur has experienced failure.

Every investor has made poor decisions. Every author has written pages that required rewriting. Every inventor has produced ideas that did not work as expected. Failure is rarely the opposite of success; more often, it is part of the path leading toward it. Those who learn from mistakes develop wisdom that cannot be purchased. Instead of asking, *"Why did this happen to me?"* they ask, *"What can this experience teach me?"* That question transforms setbacks into stepping stones.

Patience is another essential element of this mindset. Modern culture often celebrates instant results, yet meaningful wealth usually develops through gradual accumulation. Trees do not reach maturity overnight, and neither do businesses, investment portfolios, professional reputations, or intellectual property. The willingness to continue investing effort when visible progress appears slow is what separates those who quit from those who eventually succeed. **Patience is not passive waiting; it is disciplined action sustained over time while trusting the power of consistent progress.**

Gratitude also strengthens financial thinking in unexpected ways. Appreciating current resources encourages better stewardship of them. Someone who values their existing knowledge is more likely to expand it. Someone who respects their income is more likely to budget wisely. Someone who appreciates their relationships is more likely to nurture them. Gratitude shifts attention away from scarcity and toward opportunity without ignoring legitimate financial goals. It encourages thoughtful decision-making instead of impulsive comparison with others. A grateful perspective creates emotional stability, which often supports wiser long-term financial choices.

The quantum wealth mindset embraces lifelong curiosity. Markets evolve, technologies advance, industries transform, and new opportunities emerge continuously. Those who remain curious position themselves to recognize trends, develop valuable skills, and adapt to changing environments. They ask thoughtful questions, read broadly, seek reliable information, and remain open to improving their understanding. **Knowledge is one of the few assets that generally becomes more**

valuable when it is continuously expanded and applied with wisdom. Every lesson learned increases your ability to create value in a rapidly changing world.

Ultimately, the Quantum Wealth Principle is not about chasing money—it is about becoming the kind of person who consistently creates value, manages resources wisely, learns continuously, acts with integrity, and invests time intentionally. Financial prosperity becomes more sustainable when it grows from strong character rather than temporary circumstances. As you continue through this book, remember that your greatest investment is always yourself. Every skill you develop, every habit you strengthen, every relationship you cultivate, and every minute you intentionally invest contributes to a future that is richer not only in financial resources but also in wisdom, purpose, resilience, and lasting opportunity. **When your mindset grows, your capacity to create wealth grows with it.**

Exercise 1: Conduct Your Personal Time Wealth Audit

The purpose of this exercise is to help you discover where your most valuable asset—your time—is currently being invested. Many people know where their money goes because they review bank statements, but very few know where their hours actually go. This exercise will help you identify activities that build wealth, activities that simply maintain your current lifestyle, and activities that quietly consume valuable time without producing meaningful results.

Step 1: Record an Entire Day

Choose one normal day during the week. From the moment you wake up until you go to sleep, write down every activity you perform. Record activities in 15- to 30-minute increments if possible. Include work, meals, commuting, entertainment, conversations, household chores, exercise, learning, and relaxation.

Step 2: Be Completely Honest

Do not change your routine simply because you are tracking it. The goal is not to impress yourself—it is to discover the truth. Honest information creates meaningful improvement.

Step 3: Calculate the Time Spent

At the end of the day, total the amount of time spent in each major category, such as:

- Sleeping
- Working
- Learning
- Entertainment
- Social media
- Family
- Exercise
- Household responsibilities
- Personal development
- Financial planning
- Creative projects

Step 4: Highlight High-Value Activities

Use a highlighter or colored pen to mark every activity that improves your future. Examples include:

- Reading educational material
- Writing
- Building a business
- Studying investing
- Learning new skills
- Networking
- Budgeting
- Planning future goals

These activities represent investments rather than expenses of time.

Step 5: Identify Low-Value Activities

Circle activities that provided little lasting benefit. These might include excessive scrolling, unnecessary television, repetitive internet browsing, procrastination, or other habits that consumed time without helping you move closer to your goals.

Step 6: Ask the Wealth Question

For every activity, ask yourself:

"If I repeated this activity every day for the next five years, would it improve my financial future?"

Write your answer beside each activity.

Step 7: Look for Hidden Time

Search for ten- to twenty-minute periods that disappear during the day. Waiting rooms, lunch breaks, commuting (when safe), or idle moments often become opportunities for reading, planning, learning, or brainstorming.

Step 8: Choose One Activity to Reduce

Select one low-value activity that you can realistically shorten by ten minutes each day. The goal is not perfection but gradual improvement.

Step 9: Reinvest Those Ten Minutes

Immediately assign those recovered ten minutes to a wealth-building activity such as:

- Reading a chapter from a finance book
- Writing one page
- Researching investments
- Learning a new professional skill
- Planning business ideas
- Reviewing your budget
- Studying marketing
- Practicing communication or leadership

Treat this appointment with yourself as non-negotiable.

Step 10: Repeat for Seven Consecutive Days

Conduct this audit every day for one week. Patterns will begin to emerge that may not be visible after only one day.

Step 11: Reflect on the Results

At the end of the week, answer these questions:

- Which activities consistently moved me toward my goals?
- Which habits repeatedly distracted me?
- Where did I discover unexpected free time?
- What surprised me the most?

Write your observations in a notebook or journal.

Step 12: Create Your Personal Time Investment Plan

Using everything you learned, create a simple daily commitment for the next thirty days.

Complete the following statement:

"Every day, I will intentionally invest at least ten uninterrupted minutes in activities that increase my knowledge, strengthen my skills, create value for others, or improve my long-term financial future."

Review this commitment every morning before beginning your day.

Why This Exercise Matters

Most people budget their money but never budget their time. Yet **time is the resource from which all future income, opportunities, relationships, knowledge, and wealth are created**. By learning where your hours truly go, you gain the ability to redirect them toward activities that compound in value. Small adjustments made consistently can produce extraordinary long-term results, making this one of the most powerful habits you can develop throughout your financial journey.

Journal Prompts

1. What does **time is my greatest currency** personally mean to me?
2. Which daily habits are helping me build long-term wealth, and which ones are holding me back?
3. Where do I currently spend the most time that provides the least long-term value?
4. If I invested just ten focused minutes every day for the next year, what skill would have the greatest impact on my future?
5. What is one financial opportunity I have overlooked because I believed I did not have enough time?
6. How can I better align my daily schedule with the person I want to become five years from now?
7. Which knowledge or skill would increase my ability to create greater value for others?
8. What distractions consume my attention most often, and what practical steps can I take to reduce them?
9. Looking back over the past year, which investment of my time produced the greatest return in my life?
10. Beginning today, what one commitment will I make to honor my time as my most valuable asset?

Closing Reflection

Every fortune, every business, every invention, every published book, every meaningful career, and every lasting legacy began with someone choosing to invest time wisely. Before wealth appeared in a bank account, it first existed as an idea, a plan, a lesson learned, a skill practiced, or a problem solved. Money is simply one of the many results that can grow from intentional action.

The Quantum Wealth Principle reminds us that **time is the one resource distributed equally to every person, yet invested differently by each individual**. You cannot control yesterday's hours, and tomorrow has not yet arrived. The only time you truly possess is the present moment. Every decision you make today quietly shapes the opportunities available to you tomorrow.

As you continue through *Quantum Cashflow*, remember that meaningful financial success is rarely built through dramatic overnight transformations. It is built through consistent daily choices that compound over weeks, months, and years. Protect your time with the same care you would protect your greatest financial investment. Continue learning. Continue creating. Continue solving problems. Continue increasing the value you bring to others.

The future you desire is not created all at once—it is created one focused minute, one disciplined habit, and one intentional decision at a time.

Chapter 2: The 10-Minute Cashflow Formula—The Fastest Way to Generate Infinite Money

---

The Power of Ten Intentional Minutes

Most people assume that building wealth requires large amounts of free time, significant financial resources, or extraordinary talent. Because of this belief, they postpone taking meaningful action until they feel "ready." They tell themselves they will start investing when they earn more money, launch a business when life becomes less busy, write a book when they finally have enough uninterrupted hours, or learn a valuable skill when the timing is perfect. Unfortunately, perfect timing rarely arrives. Opportunities often belong to those who begin before they feel completely prepared. **The greatest obstacle to financial growth is often not a lack of resources but the habit of waiting.**

The 10-Minute Cashflow Formula is built upon a simple yet transformative principle: **consistent daily action creates momentum that occasional bursts of effort cannot match.** Ten focused minutes may seem insignificant when viewed in isolation, but those minutes represent something far greater than their duration. They represent discipline over procrastination, progress over perfection, and consistency over inconsistency. Every lasting financial achievement is ultimately composed of countless small actions repeated faithfully over time. What appears insignificant today can become extraordinary through repetition.

The word *cashflow* is often associated solely with businesses or investments, but its meaning is much broader. Cashflow represents the movement of value through your life. Money flows toward products that solve problems, services that improve lives, ideas that inspire others, and skills that organizations find valuable. The faster you become at creating meaningful value, the greater your potential for generating sustainable cashflow. This book does not suggest that money appears magically or without effort. Instead, it demonstrates that **small, intentional investments of focused time can steadily increase your**

ability to create opportunities that eventually produce financial rewards.

Ten minutes is intentionally short. Most people can find ten uninterrupted minutes regardless of how busy their schedules may seem. Because the commitment feels manageable, it becomes easier to begin. Psychology teaches us that starting is often the hardest part of any meaningful task. Once momentum begins, however, continuing becomes much easier. Many writers who intend to write for only ten minutes discover themselves working for an hour because they successfully overcame the resistance to getting started. The formula is not designed to limit your productivity—it is designed to eliminate excuses that prevent productivity from beginning.

Imagine dedicating ten focused minutes every morning to improving one aspect of your financial future. One day you may study investing principles. The next day you may outline a business idea. Another day you might improve your marketing knowledge, research industry trends, write part of a future book, organize financial records, strengthen your professional skills, or evaluate new opportunities. Individually, these sessions may appear small. Collectively, they become hundreds of purposeful decisions that gradually reshape your financial knowledge, confidence, and capabilities. **Success is often the result of ordinary actions performed with extraordinary consistency.**

The effectiveness of the formula depends upon intentional focus rather than simple activity. There is an important difference between being busy and being productive. A person may spend hours switching between emails, social media, meetings, and distractions without making meaningful progress toward long-term goals. Another individual may spend ten uninterrupted minutes concentrating completely on one high-value task and accomplish something that creates opportunities lasting for years. **Focused attention transforms limited time into meaningful progress.** Protecting those ten minutes from interruptions greatly increases their value.

The formula also encourages continuous learning rather than immediate mastery. Many people hesitate because they believe they must know everything before beginning. In reality, wealth is often built by individuals who are willing to learn while taking thoughtful action. Every ten-minute session becomes another opportunity to improve your understanding, refine your skills, correct mistakes, and discover new possibilities. Knowledge accumulates much like compound interest—the more consistently it grows, the greater its long-term value. Small daily improvements eventually create expertise that once seemed impossible.

As you begin applying the 10-Minute Cashflow Formula, remember that its greatest strength lies not in the length of each session but in the commitment behind it. Every day you choose to protect ten focused minutes, you reinforce the identity of someone who invests in the future instead of merely reacting to the present. Those minutes become appointments with your future self—moments dedicated to building knowledge, creating value, recognizing opportunity, and strengthening financial wisdom. **The journey toward lasting wealth rarely begins with a giant leap; it begins with the simple decision to invest the next ten minutes wisely.**

The Daily Cashflow Cycle

One of the reasons many people struggle financially is not because they lack intelligence or ambition, but because they lack a repeatable daily system for creating opportunities. They wake up reacting to emails, responsibilities, interruptions, and unexpected events, allowing the day to dictate their priorities. By evening, they have been busy for hours but have made little measurable progress toward improving their financial future. **The 10-Minute Cashflow Formula introduces a simple daily cycle that places intentional wealth-building at the beginning of every day rather than hoping time remains after everything else is finished.**

The Daily Cashflow Cycle consists of four connected stages: **Learn, Create, Improve, and Review.** These stages can each be practiced during separate ten-minute sessions or combined into longer periods when additional time is available. Learning expands your knowledge. Creating transforms knowledge into value. Improving strengthens the quality of what you have already built. Reviewing allows you to measure results, identify lessons, and adjust your direction. By repeating this cycle consistently, you avoid becoming stagnant because every day contributes to both personal growth and financial progress.

The first stage, **Learn**, is the fuel that powers every other stage. No industry remains unchanged forever. Technologies evolve, customer expectations shift, markets fluctuate, and new opportunities appear continuously. Spending ten focused minutes reading industry publications, studying investing principles, learning marketing strategies, understanding artificial intelligence, improving communication skills, or exploring emerging trends keeps your knowledge current. **Knowledge reduces uncertainty, and reduced uncertainty leads to better decisions.** Every lesson learned today becomes a tool you can apply tomorrow.

The second stage, **Create**, transforms information into something useful. Knowledge alone does not generate cashflow until it is applied. During this stage, you focus on producing value. You might write part of a book, design a digital product, develop software, outline a business plan, create educational material, improve a service, draft marketing content, or build systems that solve real problems. Creation is where ideas leave the imagination and begin taking practical form. Even if only one small task is completed during your ten minutes, you have moved your project forward. **Progress is measured by completed actions, not simply by accumulated ideas.**

The third stage, **Improve**, recognizes that excellence is rarely achieved on the first attempt. Every successful business, product, investment strategy, or creative work benefits from thoughtful refinement. During these sessions, you edit, simplify, strengthen, organize, and optimize what you have already created. Authors revise manuscripts. Entrepreneurs improve customer experiences. Investors refine portfolios based on research. Professionals strengthen presentations and communication. Continuous improvement allows ordinary work to gradually become exceptional. **Small refinements repeated consistently often produce remarkable increases in long-term value.**

The fourth stage, **Review**, is frequently overlooked but incredibly important. Reflection transforms experience into wisdom. At the end of each day or week, take ten minutes to evaluate your progress honestly. Ask yourself what worked well, what obstacles appeared, what lessons you learned, and what should be adjusted moving forward. Did today's work move you closer to your long-term goals? Which activities created the greatest value? Which distractions consumed unnecessary time? This process helps prevent repeating avoidable mistakes while reinforcing productive habits. **Regular review converts daily experience into lasting knowledge.**

Another strength of the Daily Cashflow Cycle is its flexibility. Some days you may spend all ten minutes learning because you are entering a new field. Other days you may focus entirely on creating because inspiration is flowing. During periods of refinement, improvement becomes the priority. Before major decisions, review may deserve greater attention. The cycle is not rigid; it adapts to your circumstances while ensuring that all four elements receive consistent attention over time. This flexibility makes the formula sustainable regardless of your profession, schedule, or financial goals.

As you continue applying the Daily Cashflow Cycle, remember that lasting wealth is built through deliberate repetition rather than isolated moments of inspiration. Every day you learn something valuable, create something useful, improve something meaningful, and review your progress, you strengthen the foundation of your future financial success. Eventually, these practices become habits, and those habits become part of your identity. **People who consistently create wealth rarely rely on motivation alone—they rely on disciplined systems that make progress inevitable one day at a time.**

Recognizing Opportunities Before Everyone Else

One of the most valuable financial skills you can develop is the ability to recognize opportunity before it becomes obvious to everyone else. Many people believe successful entrepreneurs, investors, and creators simply have extraordinary luck. While chance occasionally plays a role, lasting success is usually the result of observation, preparation, curiosity, and consistent learning. **Opportunities rarely arrive wearing a sign that says, "This will make you wealthy."** More often, they appear as ordinary problems waiting for thoughtful solutions, changing trends waiting to be understood, or unmet needs waiting for someone willing to create value.

The 10-Minute Cashflow Formula trains your mind to become an opportunity seeker rather than merely an opportunity observer. Every day you dedicate focused time to learning, researching, and creating, you begin noticing patterns that previously escaped your attention. You may identify industries experiencing rapid growth, recognize common frustrations customers repeatedly express, or discover technologies that simplify complicated tasks. The more knowledge you accumulate, the easier it becomes to connect seemingly unrelated ideas into valuable innovations. **Preparation sharpens perception, allowing you to see possibilities that others overlook.**

Many profitable ideas begin with a simple question: **"Why is this so difficult?"** Every inconvenience represents a potential opportunity. Long lines inspire faster services. Complicated software encourages simpler alternatives. Confusing educational materials create demand for clearer instruction. Expensive products motivate affordable innovations. Time-consuming processes invite automation. Rather than becoming frustrated by problems, successful wealth creators learn to become fascinated by them. Every challenge solved improves life for someone else while creating the possibility of sustainable cashflow for the individual providing the solution.

Curiosity is one of the greatest engines of opportunity recognition. Curious people constantly ask questions. They explore unfamiliar subjects, study different industries, read broadly, and remain open to ideas outside their primary field of expertise. This broad perspective often leads to unexpected breakthroughs because innovation frequently occurs where different disciplines intersect. An educator may borrow techniques from entertainment. A business owner may apply ideas from psychology. A designer may learn from architecture. A healthcare professional may adopt technology developed for another industry. **Innovation often begins when existing knowledge is viewed through a fresh perspective.**

Listening carefully is another essential habit. Customers frequently explain exactly what they need, although not always directly. Friends discuss recurring frustrations. Colleagues mention inefficient systems. Communities express concerns about products, services, or experiences. Online reviews reveal both satisfaction and disappointment. Rather than dismissing these conversations as ordinary complaints, train yourself to hear them as valuable market research. Every repeated complaint represents evidence of a problem affecting multiple people. The person who develops an effective solution creates genuine value while opening the door to financial opportunity.

Equally important is learning to evaluate opportunities objectively rather than emotionally. Not every exciting idea becomes a successful venture, and not every trend develops into a lasting market. Before committing significant time or resources, ask thoughtful questions. Does this solve a meaningful problem? Is there consistent demand? Can the solution be delivered efficiently? Does it align with my skills or interests? Can it continue creating value over time? **Careful evaluation protects your time, energy, and financial resources while increasing the likelihood of pursuing opportunities with lasting potential.**

Another principle of opportunity recognition is understanding that timing matters. An excellent idea introduced too early may struggle because the market is not ready. Introduced too late, it may face overwhelming competition. Staying informed through continuous learning allows you to recognize emerging trends before they become saturated.

However, timing should never become an excuse for endless waiting. There comes a point where preparation must give way to thoughtful action. Those who consistently create wealth understand that informed action almost always teaches more than endless speculation.

As you continue applying the 10-Minute Cashflow Formula, dedicate part of your daily practice to observing the world with fresh eyes. Ask questions others ignore. Pay attention to recurring frustrations. Study changing technologies. Listen carefully to people's needs. Explore industries beyond your own. Record ideas as they occur, no matter how small they seem. Many remarkable businesses, bestselling books, life-changing inventions, and innovative services began as simple observations made by individuals who refused to overlook everyday problems. **The next great opportunity may already exist around you—it simply requires a prepared mind willing to recognize it before everyone else does.**

Building a Lifetime of Expanding Cashflow

The true purpose of the 10-Minute Cashflow Formula is not simply to help you earn more money this month or even this year. Its greater purpose is to help you build a financial life that continues expanding through knowledge, discipline, adaptability, and value creation. Income can rise and fall throughout different seasons of life, but the ability to create value is a skill that can continue growing for decades. **Your greatest financial security does not come from a single paycheck or investment—it comes from your continually increasing capacity to solve problems, serve others, and recognize new opportunities.**

Many people think of wealth as a destination, imagining that one day they will reach a certain income level and finally consider themselves successful. In reality, lasting prosperity is much more dynamic. Markets evolve, technologies advance, industries transform, and customer needs change over time. The individuals who remain financially resilient are those who never stop learning. They understand that every year offers new lessons, new skills, and new opportunities for growth. Rather than fearing change, they prepare for it by remaining curious and adaptable. **The willingness to continue growing is one of the most valuable financial habits you can cultivate.**

An expanding cashflow is often built through diversification. This does not necessarily mean pursuing dozens of unrelated projects simultaneously. Instead, it means developing multiple ways to create value over time. Someone may earn income through employment while gradually publishing books, investing responsibly, developing educational resources, licensing creative work, consulting within their area of expertise, or building a business. Each additional source of value strengthens overall financial stability because success no longer depends entirely on a single stream of income. Thoughtful diversification increases resilience without sacrificing focus.

Equally important is protecting the cashflow you create. Generating income is only one part of financial success; managing it wisely is equally essential. Budgeting, saving, investing prudently, reducing unnecessary debt, maintaining emergency reserves, and making informed financial decisions help ensure that today's opportunities contribute to tomorrow's security. A growing income combined with disciplined financial stewardship creates a foundation capable of supporting long-term goals. **Money that is managed with intention becomes a tool for creating greater freedom, greater opportunity, and greater peace of mind.**

The 10-Minute Cashflow Formula also reminds us that relationships play an essential role in lasting prosperity. Financial growth is rarely achieved in complete isolation. Mentors provide guidance, collaborators contribute complementary strengths, clients create opportunities, readers support authors, customers sustain businesses, and communities encourage continued improvement. Every interaction becomes an opportunity to build trust through integrity, reliability, professionalism, and genuine service. A strong reputation often opens doors that money alone cannot. **Character remains one of the most valuable assets in every economy because trust cannot be manufactured overnight.**

As your knowledge and resources grow, another responsibility emerges: helping others grow as well. Teaching, mentoring, encouraging, and sharing useful insights strengthen both individuals and communities. Every successful person once benefited from someone willing to share experience, answer questions, or provide encouragement during uncertain moments. Contributing to the success of others does not diminish your own opportunities; in many cases, it expands them by creating stronger networks, deeper relationships, and a reputation for generosity and leadership. Wealth becomes more meaningful when it is used to improve lives beyond your own.

Throughout this chapter, one central idea has remained constant: meaningful progress is built through consistent daily investment rather than occasional extraordinary effort. Every ten-minute session devoted to learning, creating, improving, reviewing, or recognizing opportunities becomes another brick in the foundation of your future. The cumulative effect may be invisible at first, but over months and years those small investments develop into knowledge, assets, systems, confidence, and opportunities that would have seemed impossible at the beginning. **Never underestimate the extraordinary power of ordinary consistency.**

As you prepare to move into the next chapter, remember that the 10-Minute Cashflow Formula is far more than a productivity technique—it is a philosophy of intentional living. Every day presents a fresh opportunity to learn something valuable, create something meaningful, improve something useful, strengthen a relationship, and move one step closer to your long-term vision. The amount of time required is modest, but the potential impact is enormous. Protect those ten minutes with determination. Invest them with purpose. Repeat the process faithfully. Over time, you will discover that **lasting wealth is not created by dramatic moments of inspiration alone—it is built through thousands of intentional decisions that quietly compound into a lifetime of expanding opportunity, enduring value, and sustainable cashflow.**

Exercise 1: Build Your Personal 10-Minute Cashflow Routine

The purpose of this exercise is to create a practical daily routine that transforms ten focused minutes into a consistent wealth-building habit. The objective is not to become wealthy overnight but to establish a repeatable system that increases your knowledge, creates valuable assets, and strengthens your long-term financial opportunities. By following these steps consistently, you begin replacing random financial effort with intentional daily progress.

Step 1: Define Your Primary Financial Goal

Write one clear financial objective that you want to accomplish over the next twelve months.

Examples include:

- Publish your first book.
- Start a small business.
- Eliminate a specific debt.
- Build an emergency fund.
- Learn investing.
- Increase your monthly income.
- Develop a second source of income.

Your goal should be specific enough that you can measure your progress.

Step 2: Write Your "Why"
Below your goal, explain why achieving it matters.
Ask yourself:

- How will this improve my life?
- Who will benefit besides me?
- What opportunities will this create?

A meaningful reason provides motivation when enthusiasm naturally rises and falls.

Step 3: Select Your Daily Ten Minutes
Choose one consistent time every day.
Examples include:

- Immediately after waking up.
- During lunch.
- Before work.
- After dinner.
- Thirty minutes before bedtime.

Protect this appointment exactly as you would an important business meeting.

Step 4: Remove Every Distraction

Before beginning your session:

- Silence your phone.
- Close unnecessary browser tabs.
- Turn off television.
- Place your phone out of reach if possible.
- Inform family members that you need ten uninterrupted minutes.

Your attention is your greatest investment.

Step 5: Choose One High-Value Activity
Select only one task.
Examples include:

- Research a market.
- Write one page.
- Learn investing.
- Study marketing.
- Build your website.
- Improve your résumé.
- Learn AI tools.
- Create product ideas.
- Read one chapter of a financial book.
- Analyze business opportunities.

Do not multitask.

Step 6: Set a Ten-Minute Timer

Start a timer and commit to working without interruption until it expires.

Avoid checking notifications, email, or social media.

Focus completely on your selected task.

Step 7: Record What You Completed

Immediately after finishing, write down:

- Today's date.
- The task completed.
- One thing you learned.
- One next step for tomorrow.

Even small accomplishments deserve to be documented because progress compounds.

Step 8: Identify One Improvement

Ask yourself:

"How can I make tomorrow's ten minutes even more productive?"

Perhaps you need better preparation, fewer distractions, improved organization, or clearer priorities.

Continuous improvement is part of the formula.

Step 9: Celebrate Consistency

Do not measure success only by money earned.

Instead, celebrate:

- Showing up.
- Keeping your promise.
- Completing today's session.
- Learning something new.
- Building momentum.

Consistency deserves recognition because it creates extraordinary long-term results.

Step 10: Repeat for Thirty Consecutive Days

Commit to completing your ten-minute session every day for one month.

Do not worry about perfection.

If you miss one day, begin again immediately without discouragement.

The goal is building a lifelong habit.

Step 11: Evaluate Your Growth

After thirty days, review your journal and answer:

- What have I created?
- What have I learned?
- Which habits became easier?
- Which distractions became smaller?
- How has my confidence changed?

Notice improvements beyond finances, including discipline, focus, and organization.

Step 12: Expand When Ready

Once your ten-minute habit feels automatic, consider increasing your focused work to twenty or thirty minutes on days when your schedule allows.

Never abandon the ten-minute commitment.

It remains your minimum daily investment in your future, ensuring that progress continues regardless of how busy life becomes.

Why This Exercise Matters

The greatest purpose of this exercise is not to teach time management—it is to help you become the type of person who consistently invests in the future. Every completed session strengthens discipline, builds confidence, increases knowledge, and creates momentum. Over weeks, months, and years, those seemingly modest investments accumulate into skills, assets, opportunities, and financial wisdom that continue producing value long after the original ten minutes have passed. **Small daily actions, faithfully repeated, have the power to reshape an entire financial future.**

Journal Prompts

1. What financial goal would have the greatest positive impact on my life if I devoted just ten focused minutes to it every day for the next year?
2. Which excuses have I been using to delay taking action, and how can the 10-Minute Cashflow Formula help me overcome them?
3. What knowledge or skill would most increase my ability to create value for others?
4. Which of my current habits contribute to building long-term cashflow, and which habits quietly reduce my productivity?
5. If I could create one income-producing asset over the next twelve months, what would it be, and why?
6. What problems do I regularly notice in my personal life, workplace, or community that could become opportunities to create value?
7. How can I better protect my daily ten-minute wealth-building appointment from distractions and interruptions?
8. Looking back at this chapter, which idea challenged my current thinking about money, productivity, or opportunity the most?
9. What specific action will I take within the next twenty-four hours to begin applying the 10-Minute Cashflow Formula?
10. One year from today, if I remain faithful to investing ten focused minutes every day, what do I hope my financial life, knowledge, confidence, and opportunities will look like?

Closing Reflection

The 10-Minute Cashflow Formula is built upon a simple but powerful truth: **lasting wealth is rarely the result of one extraordinary decision—it is the result of thousands of intentional decisions made consistently over time.** Every meaningful financial achievement begins long before money is earned. It begins when you choose to invest your attention, protect your time, develop valuable skills, and create something that improves the lives of others.

Throughout this chapter, you discovered that ten focused minutes can become far more valuable than hours of distracted activity. Those brief daily sessions allow you to learn continuously, create meaningful assets, recognize opportunities, strengthen your financial knowledge, and build habits that compound throughout your lifetime. While each session may seem modest on its own, together they form a system capable of producing extraordinary long-term results.

Remember that **cashflow begins with value, and value begins with intentional action.** Every page you write, every lesson you study, every system you improve, every relationship you strengthen, and every problem you solve increases your capacity to create opportunities. Financial growth becomes the natural result of consistently increasing the value you contribute to the world.

As you move into the next chapter, make one commitment to yourself: never underestimate the power of today's ten minutes. Protect them with purpose. Invest them with discipline. Repeat the process with patience. There will be days when progress feels slow and results seem invisible, but those are often the very days when your future is being built most profoundly. **Small actions become lasting habits, lasting habits become powerful systems, and powerful systems become the foundation of enduring wealth.**

The journey toward financial freedom is not won in a single moment. It is won one focused decision, one valuable lesson, one completed task, and one intentional ten-minute investment at a time.

Chapter 3: Hacking Perception—How to Become a Money Magnet Instantly

---

The Lens Through Which You See Opportunity

Every person views the world through an invisible lens shaped by past experiences, beliefs, education, habits, and expectations. This mental lens influences how opportunities are recognized, how risks are evaluated, and how decisions are made. Two individuals can stand in the same room, witness the same event, and leave with completely different conclusions. One may see limitations, uncertainty, and reasons to wait, while the other notices unmet needs, valuable connections, and possibilities for growth. **Your perception influences what you notice long before it influences what you achieve.** The ability to reshape that perception is one of the most valuable financial skills you can develop.

The phrase **"money magnet"** should not be understood as a mystical force that attracts wealth without effort or responsibility. Throughout this book, it represents a mindset and pattern of behavior that naturally increases your ability to recognize, create, and respond to opportunities that produce value. People who consistently generate wealth often appear fortunate, but closer examination usually reveals years of observation, preparation, disciplined action, and continuous learning. Their perception has been trained to notice possibilities that others overlook because they have developed the habit of looking for solutions instead of obstacles.

Your brain constantly filters enormous amounts of information. Every second, your senses receive more input than your conscious mind can process, so your brain determines what deserves attention. This filtering system is influenced by what you repeatedly think about and consider important. Someone passionate about architecture notices unique buildings almost everywhere. A musician hears subtle details in songs that others may never recognize. An experienced investor may detect important economic trends hidden within ordinary news reports. Likewise, someone who intentionally trains themselves to recognize opportunities begins seeing ideas, connections, and solutions that previously passed unnoticed. **Where your attention consistently goes, your awareness naturally follows.**

One of the fastest ways to improve financial perception is to replace passive observation with active curiosity. Rather than asking, "What happened today?" begin asking questions such as, **"What problem needs solving?"**, **"Why does this process seem inefficient?"**, **"How could this service be improved?"**, or **"What skill would make this task easier?"** These questions encourage your mind to search for constructive answers instead of simply accepting situations as they appear. Curiosity transforms everyday experiences into opportunities for learning, innovation, and value creation.

Perception is also shaped by the language you use when speaking to yourself. Internal conversations influence confidence, resilience, and willingness to act. A person who repeatedly says, "I'm terrible with money," or "Opportunities never come my way," reinforces beliefs that discourage growth and exploration. In contrast, someone who asks, **"What can I learn from this?"**, **"How can I improve?"**, or **"Where is the opportunity hidden within this challenge?"** directs attention toward constructive action. While positive thinking alone does not create wealth, **constructive thinking encourages behaviors that increase the likelihood of discovering meaningful opportunities.**

Another important aspect of perception involves separating temporary setbacks from permanent conclusions. Every entrepreneur experiences rejection. Every investor encounters periods of uncertainty. Every creator produces work that requires improvement. These moments do not define future potential unless they are interpreted as evidence that growth is impossible. Individuals with healthy financial perception view setbacks as information rather than identity. They ask what can be improved, adjusted, or learned instead of assuming one disappointment determines the outcome of an entire journey. **Resilient perception transforms mistakes into education rather than discouragement.**

Developing stronger perception also requires surrounding yourself with high-quality information. The books you read, the conversations you have, the mentors you seek, and the educational resources you choose all influence how you interpret the world. Filling your mind with thoughtful ideas, reliable knowledge, practical wisdom, and diverse perspectives gradually reshapes the questions you ask and the opportunities you recognize. Just as nutritious food strengthens the body, valuable information strengthens the quality of your decisions. **Your environment quietly influences your perception every single day. Choose it intentionally.**

As you begin this chapter, remember that changing your financial future often begins with changing what you notice. Opportunities rarely appear overnight; they become visible because your perception has evolved enough to recognize them. Every day you train yourself to ask better questions, seek practical knowledge, remain curious, and focus on creating value, your awareness expands. **The world around you may remain exactly the same, but your ability to recognize possibility within it can change dramatically. That shift in perception is where lasting financial transformation begins.**

Reprogramming Your Financial Beliefs

Every financial decision you make is influenced by beliefs that have been forming throughout your entire life. Some of these beliefs were taught directly by parents, teachers, mentors, or friends. Others developed quietly through personal experiences, cultural influences, media, and observation. Many people never stop to examine whether these beliefs are accurate or useful—they simply accept them as facts. Yet some of the most powerful barriers to financial growth exist not in the economy, but in the assumptions people unknowingly carry about money, success, and opportunity. **Before changing your financial results, you must first examine the beliefs that influence your financial decisions.**

Financial beliefs are often formed long before a person earns their first paycheck. A child who repeatedly hears phrases such as "Money doesn't grow on trees," "Rich people are dishonest," "You'll never get ahead," or "People like us don't become wealthy," may unconsciously carry those messages into adulthood. Although many of these statements were originally intended to teach responsibility or caution, they can sometimes create limiting assumptions if accepted without reflection. Conversely, someone raised to believe that education, integrity, hard work, and continuous learning create opportunities may approach financial challenges with greater confidence and optimism. **Beliefs influence expectations, and expectations often influence behavior.**

One effective way to strengthen your financial mindset is to distinguish between facts and assumptions. A fact can be supported by objective evidence. An assumption is an interpretation that may or may not be true. For example, "Learning new skills takes time" is a fact. "I'm too old to learn something valuable" is an assumption. "Markets experience periods of growth and decline" is a fact. "I'll never understand investing" is an assumption. When limiting beliefs are identified as assumptions rather than permanent truths, they become open to examination and improvement. This shift encourages growth rather than resignation.

Another important practice is replacing unproductive questions with constructive ones. The questions you repeatedly ask yourself determine where your attention is directed. Asking, "Why does nothing ever work for me?" encourages the mind to search for evidence supporting discouragement. Asking, **"What can I learn from this experience?"** or **"What is one practical step I can take today?"** encourages solution-oriented thinking. The purpose is not to ignore challenges but to respond to them with curiosity and responsibility instead of helplessness. **Better questions often produce better decisions because they encourage better thinking.**

Confidence also grows through evidence rather than wishful thinking. Every small success reinforces the belief that additional progress is possible. Completing a financial course, saving the first hundred dollars toward an emergency fund, publishing a first article, learning a new professional skill, or creating a simple digital product all provide tangible proof that growth is occurring. These experiences gradually replace uncertainty with confidence because they are supported by action. **Lasting confidence is built through consistent achievement, no matter how modest the beginning may seem.**

Reprogramming financial beliefs also requires becoming comfortable with continuous learning. The economy changes. Technologies evolve. Industries transform. New investment options emerge while others become less effective. Individuals who remain adaptable avoid becoming trapped by outdated assumptions. Instead of believing they already know everything necessary, they maintain the attitude of lifelong students. This humility keeps their knowledge current while increasing their ability to recognize new opportunities. **An open mind is often one of the greatest competitive advantages in a rapidly changing world.**

Equally important is recognizing that financial success and personal integrity can exist together. Some people mistakenly believe that prosperity requires sacrificing ethics, compassion, or honesty. In reality, many enduring businesses, respected professionals, and successful investors build their reputations by consistently delivering value while acting responsibly. Trust becomes an asset that attracts clients, customers, partnerships, and opportunities over many years. Wealth built through integrity is often more sustainable because it is supported by strong relationships and a positive reputation. **Character strengthens opportunity by creating confidence in those who choose to work with you.**

As you continue developing the Quantum Wealth mindset, remember that beliefs are not fixed characteristics—they are frameworks that can be strengthened through education, thoughtful reflection, and consistent action. Each time you replace a limiting assumption with a practical strategy, each time you ask a better question, and each time you take one meaningful step forward, you reshape the way you perceive yourself and your opportunities. **Your financial future is influenced not only by what you know today but also by what you choose to believe is possible through continuous learning, disciplined action, and the steady creation of value.**

Training Your Mind to Recognize Value Everywhere

One of the defining characteristics of financially successful people is that they develop the habit of recognizing value where others see only ordinary circumstances. This does not mean they believe every idea will become profitable or that every opportunity will lead to success. Instead, they train themselves to observe the world with curiosity, asking how products, services, systems, relationships, and knowledge can be improved. **The ability to recognize value is often more important than the ability to recognize money, because money generally follows value that consistently serves others.**

Value exists wherever problems exist. Every inconvenience, inefficiency, unanswered question, or unmet need represents the possibility of creating something useful. A long wait for customer service may inspire a faster communication system. Confusing software may encourage someone to design a simpler interface. A lack of educational resources may motivate an expert to write a book or create an online course. Everyday frustrations often become the starting point for meaningful innovation. Instead of becoming discouraged by problems, begin asking, **"What solution would make this easier?"** That single question has inspired countless businesses, inventions, and creative projects throughout history.

Another way to strengthen your perception is by becoming an intentional observer. Carry a notebook or use a digital note-taking application to record interesting ideas throughout the day. Write down recurring complaints you hear from friends, coworkers, customers, or family members. Record interesting trends, business concepts, articles, technologies, and questions that spark your curiosity. Most ideas may never become businesses, but consistently capturing observations trains your brain to remain alert rather than passive. **A prepared mind notices opportunities because it has developed the habit of paying attention.**

Value also exists within your own experiences. Every challenge you have overcome has taught you something. Every profession you have worked in has given you practical knowledge. Every hobby has developed skills. Every personal success and setback has expanded your understanding in unique ways. Often, people underestimate the value of what they already know because it feels familiar. Yet someone else who has never faced the same challenge may greatly benefit from your experience. Books, workshops, consulting, coaching, educational resources, digital products, and creative services frequently begin with knowledge that the creator once considered ordinary.

Recognizing value requires developing empathy as well as observation. Instead of focusing exclusively on what interests you, learn to understand what matters to other people. What are they trying to accomplish? What obstacles slow them down? What information are they searching for? What experiences do they wish were simpler, faster, safer, or more enjoyable? The more clearly you understand the needs of others, the more effectively you can create solutions that genuinely improve their lives. **Lasting financial success is built by serving people well rather than simply attempting to sell something.**

The modern world provides extraordinary opportunities for observing value because information is more accessible than ever before. Customer reviews reveal what people appreciate and what frustrates them. Industry reports identify changing trends. Educational resources explain emerging technologies. Community discussions highlight recurring concerns. Marketplaces reveal products people purchase repeatedly. By spending even ten focused minutes each day studying these sources thoughtfully, you steadily improve your ability to recognize where meaningful opportunities may exist. Knowledge gathered consistently becomes a powerful advantage over time.

It is equally important to evaluate opportunities with patience and discernment. Not every idea deserves immediate action. Some concepts require additional research, testing, refinement, or validation before significant resources are invested. Ask yourself whether the problem is widespread, whether your proposed solution provides genuine improvement, and whether you possess—or can realistically develop—the skills needed to deliver it effectively. **Careful evaluation protects your time while increasing the likelihood that your efforts will be directed toward opportunities with lasting potential.**

As you continue strengthening your financial perception, remember that value is rarely hidden—it is simply overlooked by those who have not trained themselves to recognize it. Every conversation, every challenge, every article, every customer experience, every technological advance, and every ordinary day contains lessons waiting to be discovered. The more intentionally you observe the world, the more opportunities you will begin to notice. Over time, this habit becomes second nature, allowing you to see possibilities where others see routine. **When you consistently learn to recognize value everywhere, you dramatically increase your ability to create meaningful opportunities that benefit both others and yourself.**

The Habits That Naturally Attract Opportunity

People often describe successful individuals as being "in the right place at the right time." While timing can certainly influence outcomes, what appears to be luck is frequently the result of habits that quietly position a person to recognize and act upon opportunities. Opportunities rarely arrive because someone wishes for them—they more often appear because someone has consistently prepared, learned, built relationships, and developed the discipline to act when the moment arrives. **The more intentionally you live, the more opportunities you are likely to recognize and pursue.**

One of the most valuable habits you can develop is reliability. Whether you are working with employers, customers, clients, readers, or business partners, consistently doing what you say you will do builds trust. Trust is one of the strongest foundations of long-term financial success because people naturally prefer to work with individuals they consider dependable. Delivering quality work on time, communicating honestly, and following through on commitments create a reputation that often generates opportunities through recommendations and repeat business. **Your reputation becomes a form of invisible capital that grows stronger with every promise you keep.**

Another opportunity-attracting habit is continuous learning. The marketplace constantly changes as technology advances, industries evolve, and consumer needs shift. Those who dedicate time each day to expanding their knowledge remain prepared for these changes instead of being surprised by them. Reading books, studying industry trends, learning new software, improving communication skills, or exploring emerging technologies all strengthen your ability to recognize opportunities before they become obvious. Every new skill increases the number of ways you can contribute value to others.

Generosity also plays an important role in building lasting opportunities. Sharing useful knowledge, helping solve problems, introducing people to valuable connections, or offering encouragement without expecting immediate rewards strengthens relationships over time. This is not about giving with the expectation of receiving something in return. Rather, it reflects the understanding that communities thrive when people contribute positively to one another's success. Individuals known for being helpful, knowledgeable, and trustworthy often become the first people others think of when new opportunities arise. **Giving value freely often creates relationships that lead to opportunities money alone cannot purchase.**

Curiosity keeps your mind open to possibilities that routine thinking may overlook. Curious individuals ask thoughtful questions instead of assuming they already know the answers. They explore unfamiliar subjects, seek diverse perspectives, and remain willing to challenge outdated assumptions. This habit often leads to innovation because it encourages connections between ideas from different fields. Whether you are an author, entrepreneur, investor, educator, or professional in any industry, curiosity expands your ability to adapt and discover creative solutions to changing circumstances.

Discipline is another habit that quietly attracts opportunity. Inspiration comes and goes, but disciplined action ensures progress continues regardless of temporary motivation. Completing your daily ten-minute session, honoring commitments, reviewing goals regularly, and steadily improving your skills demonstrate reliability both to yourself and to others. People who consistently produce quality work become known for their dependability, making them more likely to be considered when meaningful opportunities arise. **Consistency often distinguishes professionals from those who rely solely on occasional bursts of motivation.**

Equally important is maintaining a long-term perspective. Many opportunities require patience before producing measurable financial results. A book may take months to write before publication. A business may need time to establish a customer base. Investments often grow gradually over years rather than days. Skills improve through repeated practice rather than overnight transformation. Those who remain committed during periods when visible progress is limited frequently discover that persistence itself becomes a competitive advantage. **Long-term thinking allows small daily improvements to accumulate into significant achievements that short-term thinking often abandons too soon.**

Ultimately, becoming a "money magnet" is not about attracting wealth through passive hope—it is about developing habits that naturally increase your ability to recognize, create, and respond to opportunities. Reliability builds trust. Learning expands knowledge. Generosity strengthens relationships. Curiosity uncovers possibilities. Discipline produces consistent progress. Patience allows results to mature over time. Together, these habits create an environment in which opportunities become easier to recognize and better prepared to seize. **The more intentionally you develop these qualities, the more your life becomes aligned with the kinds of opportunities that support lasting financial growth and meaningful success.**

Seeing the World Through an Abundance Perspective

One of the most significant shifts a person can make in developing financial wisdom is moving from a scarcity perspective to an abundance perspective. A scarcity perspective assumes there is never enough—never enough money, opportunity, time, success, customers, ideas, or resources. This mindset often leads to fear, hesitation, unhealthy comparison, and short-term decision-making. An abundance perspective, by contrast, recognizes that while resources may sometimes be limited, opportunities to create value continue to emerge through learning, innovation, cooperation, and thoughtful action. **An abundance perspective does not ignore reality; it encourages you to look for constructive possibilities within it.**

An abundance perspective begins with recognizing that value can be created rather than merely competed over. History is filled with examples of individuals who introduced products, services, technologies, books, educational resources, and businesses that did not previously exist. They did not simply divide an existing opportunity into smaller pieces—they expanded what was available by solving problems in new ways. Every meaningful innovation demonstrates that growth is possible through creativity and service. Instead of asking, "How can I take a larger share?" begin asking, **"How can I create greater value?"** This shift encourages contribution rather than competition alone.

Comparison is one of the greatest obstacles to maintaining an abundance perspective. It is easy to become discouraged when measuring your beginning against someone else's years of experience or visible success. Social media and public recognition often highlight achievements while hiding the countless hours of learning, setbacks, revisions, and perseverance that occurred behind the scenes. Every successful author once wrote a first page. Every respected entrepreneur launched a first project. Every experienced investor made a first investment. **Your journey deserves to be measured against your own progress rather than someone else's timeline.**

Gratitude strengthens an abundance perspective because it encourages awareness of existing resources while still leaving room for growth. Appreciating your current knowledge, relationships, health, skills, experiences, and opportunities helps you become a better steward of them. Gratitude does not mean becoming complacent or abandoning ambitious goals. Instead, it creates emotional stability that supports thoughtful decision-making. Individuals who appreciate what they already possess are often better positioned to build upon those resources with wisdom and intention.

Another characteristic of an abundance perspective is collaboration. Scarcity often encourages the belief that another person's success reduces your own chances of succeeding. In many situations, the opposite is true. Partnerships, professional networks, mentorships, and collaborative projects frequently create opportunities that would have been difficult to achieve individually. Working with others who possess complementary skills often produces stronger ideas, higher-quality work, and broader opportunities. **When value is created together, everyone involved can benefit from the combined strengths of the relationship.**

Maintaining an abundance perspective also requires resilience during periods of uncertainty. Economic conditions change. Markets fluctuate. New technologies reshape industries. Unexpected challenges arise. Individuals who maintain an abundance mindset acknowledge these realities while continuing to search for practical responses. They ask, "What opportunities still exist?" "What skills should I strengthen?" and "How can I continue creating value under these circumstances?" This approach encourages adaptability rather than paralysis. Every challenge becomes an invitation to learn, adjust, and continue moving forward with purpose.

It is equally important to recognize that abundance grows through generosity, integrity, and service. People naturally remember those who contribute positively to their lives. A professional who consistently delivers quality work, an author who educates readers thoughtfully, a business owner who genuinely cares about customers, or a mentor who shares knowledge generously builds trust over time. Trust often becomes the foundation for referrals, partnerships, loyal customers, and lasting opportunities. **Character expands opportunity because people are drawn toward those they respect and trust.**

As you conclude this chapter's exploration of perception, remember that becoming a "money magnet" is fundamentally about becoming a person who consistently notices opportunities, creates meaningful value, develops reliable habits, and approaches the future with curiosity, integrity, and an abundance perspective. Money itself is not attracted by wishful thinking—it generally follows thoughtful preparation, valuable contribution, wise decisions, and consistent action. Every day offers new opportunities to strengthen your perception, improve your skills, deepen your relationships, and expand your ability to serve others. **When you train yourself to see possibility instead of limitation, value instead of scarcity, and opportunity instead of fear, you place yourself in a far stronger position to build lasting financial success.**

Exercise 1: Reframe Your Financial Perception

The purpose of this exercise is to help you become aware of the beliefs, assumptions, and thought patterns that influence your financial decisions. Rather than attempting to "think positively" without evidence, this exercise focuses on replacing limiting assumptions with practical, constructive perspectives supported by learning and action. The goal is to train your mind to recognize opportunity, value, and possibility more consistently.

Step 1: Create a Quiet Environment

Choose a location where you can think without interruption for at least twenty to thirty minutes.

Bring a notebook or journal and remove distractions such as your phone, television, or unnecessary browser tabs.

A calm environment encourages honest reflection.

Step 2: Write Down Every Financial Belief That Comes to Mind

Without judging your answers, list every statement you believe about money.

Examples include:

- Money is difficult to earn.
- Wealth requires luck.
- Successful people work harder.
- Investing is complicated.
- I can always learn new skills.
- Businesses solve problems.
- Knowledge creates opportunity.

Write everything exactly as it comes to mind.

Step 3: Separate Facts from Assumptions

Next to each statement, write either:

Fact or **Assumption**

Ask yourself:

- Can this be objectively proven?
- Is this based on evidence?
- Did I learn this from someone else?
- Have I personally tested this belief?

Many long-held beliefs become assumptions once examined carefully.

Step 4: Identify Limiting Beliefs
Circle every assumption that discourages growth.
Examples include:

- I'm too old.
- I'm too young.
- I missed my chance.
- Successful people are different from me.
- I don't know enough.

Remember:
A limiting belief is not necessarily false because it feels convincing.

Step 5: Replace Each Limiting Belief

For every limiting assumption, write a practical replacement.

Example:

Instead of:

"I'll never understand investing."

Write:

"I can improve my financial knowledge by studying a little every day."

Instead of:

"I don't have enough time."

Write:

"I can consistently invest ten focused minutes each day."

Constructive replacements encourage action rather than avoidance.

Step 6: Find Supporting Evidence
For every new belief, write at least one real example supporting it. Perhaps:

- You learned a difficult skill before.
- You completed a challenging project.
- You solved a difficult problem.
- Someone with similar circumstances succeeded.

Evidence strengthens confidence far more effectively than wishful thinking.

Step 7: Write Three Opportunity Questions
Create three questions you will ask yourself every day.
Examples:

- What problem can I solve today?
- Where is value being overlooked?
- What can I learn in the next ten minutes?

These questions train your perception to search for opportunities.

Step 8: Practice Opportunity Observation
Spend one full day intentionally observing your surroundings.
Record:

- Common complaints.
- Inefficient systems.
- Frequently asked questions.
- Customer frustrations.
- Interesting trends.

Do not attempt to solve everything immediately.
Simply learn to notice.

Step 9: Choose One Opportunity

Review your observations and select one idea with genuine potential.

Ask yourself:

- Does this solve a real problem?
- Who would benefit?
- Could I realistically contribute value?

Write a one-page description of your idea.

Step 10: Take One Small Action

Within the next twenty-four hours, complete one meaningful step. Examples:

- Research the market.
- Read an article.
- Sketch a prototype.
- Write an outline.
- Contact an expert.
- Study competitors.

Momentum begins with movement.

Step 11: Reflect on Your Thinking

Answer these questions:

- Which belief changed the most?
- Which opportunity surprised me?
- Which assumption no longer seems true?
- What did I learn about myself?

Reflection transforms experience into wisdom.

Step 12: Repeat Every Month

Return to this exercise every thirty days.

Review your beliefs again.

Notice which assumptions have disappeared, which new opportunities have emerged, and how your perception continues expanding.

Over time, you will discover that your greatest transformation often occurs not in your bank account first, but in the way you interpret the world around you.

Why This Exercise Matters

Financial growth begins with improved perception. The opportunities available to you today may not have changed—but your ability to recognize them certainly can. By questioning limiting assumptions, strengthening constructive beliefs with evidence, asking better questions, and intentionally observing the world for opportunities, you gradually train your mind to notice value that previously went unseen. **As your perception expands, so does your ability to create meaningful opportunities, make wiser decisions, and build lasting financial success.**

Journal Prompts

1. Which financial belief has had the greatest influence on my life, and where do I think that belief originated?
2. What opportunities have I overlooked in the past because I assumed they were beyond my abilities or resources?
3. How has my perception of money changed after reading this chapter?
4. What recurring problems do I notice in my daily life that could become opportunities to create value for others?
5. Which of my personal skills, experiences, or areas of knowledge could be developed into something that helps other people?
6. How can I intentionally train myself each day to notice opportunities instead of focusing on obstacles?
7. Which limiting assumption am I committed to replacing, and what practical actions will reinforce my new perspective?
8. Who are the people, books, or educational resources that most positively influence my financial thinking, and how can I spend more time learning from them?
9. Looking one year into the future, how would my life change if I consistently approached challenges with curiosity, resilience, and an abundance perspective?
10. Beginning today, what one daily habit will help me strengthen my perception, recognize more opportunities, and create greater value for others?

Closing Reflection

The greatest transformation in wealth rarely begins with a paycheck, an investment, or a business opportunity. It begins with a change in perception. Before people create something valuable, they first recognize a possibility that others fail to notice. Before they solve a problem, they choose to see the problem differently. Before they build lasting financial success, they develop the habit of looking beyond limitations and toward meaningful solutions.

Throughout this chapter, you discovered that becoming a **money magnet** is not about attracting money through wishful thinking or passive expectation. It is about cultivating a mindset that naturally recognizes value, seeks opportunities, asks better questions, strengthens useful skills, and responds to challenges with thoughtful action. As your perception improves, your decisions improve. As your decisions improve, your actions become more intentional. Over time, those intentional actions compound into greater knowledge, stronger relationships, valuable assets, and expanding financial opportunities.

Remember that your mind is constantly filtering information. Every day, countless opportunities pass by unnoticed simply because they fall outside the focus of your attention. By choosing to direct your attention toward learning, service, innovation, and value creation, you gradually train yourself to recognize possibilities that once seemed invisible. **Your greatest competitive advantage is often not having more resources than others—it is seeing potential where others see routine.**

Never underestimate the influence of small shifts in perspective. One new question can lead to a valuable idea. One observation can inspire a successful business. One conversation can open the door to a life-changing partnership. One lesson can prevent an expensive mistake. One decision to remain curious instead of discouraged can alter the direction of an entire career. The future is often shaped by moments that seemed ordinary when they first occurred.

As you move into the next chapter, continue protecting your attention, expanding your knowledge, and refining the way you view the world. Stay curious. Stay observant. Continue asking how you can create greater value for others. **When your perception grows, your opportunities grow. When your opportunities grow, your ability to create lasting wealth grows with them. Every remarkable financial journey begins by seeing what is possible before it becomes obvious to everyone else.**

Chapter 4: The 4th-Dimensional Business Model—Why Traditional Work Is Obsolete

---

Beyond Trading Time for Money

For generations, the dominant model of earning a living has been straightforward: exchange a certain number of hours for a certain amount of income. This approach helped build industries, supported families, and fueled economic growth throughout much of the modern world. Honest work remains honorable and essential, and millions of people continue to build meaningful careers through employment. However, the economic landscape has changed dramatically. Digital technology, automation, global communication, artificial intelligence, and scalable intellectual property have created entirely new ways to generate value. **The goal of this chapter is not to dismiss traditional work but to explore how value can now extend far beyond the hours directly invested.**

The phrase **"4th-Dimensional Business Model"** is used throughout this book as a metaphor for thinking beyond the traditional limitations of time and location. Rather than viewing income as something that exists only while you are actively working, this model encourages building systems, assets, and solutions that continue creating value after the original effort has been completed. A book can educate readers years after publication. Software can assist users every hour of the day. Educational resources can reach learners across the globe. A carefully designed licensing agreement can continue producing royalties over time. **The fourth dimension is not magic—it is leverage created through scalable value.**

Traditional employment generally rewards time already spent. In contrast, scalable assets have the potential to reward value that continues serving others long after it has been created. This distinction changes the way successful creators, entrepreneurs, educators, inventors, and investors think about productivity. Instead of asking, *"How many hours can I work?"* they begin asking, **"What can I build today**

that will continue helping people tomorrow?" That question encourages long-term thinking and shifts attention from temporary effort toward lasting contribution.

One of the greatest advantages of modern technology is its ability to remove many historical limitations. An author no longer needs to print thousands of physical books before reaching readers around the world. A teacher can educate students across continents through digital platforms. A designer can distribute creative work globally within minutes. A consultant can provide expertise through virtual meetings instead of geographic proximity. These developments have fundamentally expanded the ways people can share knowledge, creativity, and practical solutions. **Technology has transformed distance from a barrier into an opportunity.**

This shift also changes the relationship between effort and impact. In a purely time-based model, helping one additional customer often requires another hour of work. In a scalable model, a single well-designed solution may help hundreds or thousands of people with only periodic updates and improvements. While creating such assets frequently requires significant effort at the beginning, their long-term value lies in their ability to continue serving others efficiently. This does not eliminate hard work—it redirects hard work toward building systems that produce value repeatedly instead of only once.

The 4th-Dimensional Business Model also encourages viewing knowledge as one of your most valuable forms of capital. Every skill you develop, every lesson you learn, every process you improve, and every challenge you overcome has the potential to become useful to someone else. Knowledge can be transformed into books, educational courses, consulting services, digital tools, software, presentations, templates, research, or countless other resources. **Intellectual capital often becomes increasingly valuable when it is organized, refined, and shared effectively.**

Another important characteristic of this model is adaptability. Industries evolve continuously. Technologies improve. Consumer expectations change. Economic conditions shift. Businesses that remain successful over long periods rarely depend upon doing things exactly as they did decades earlier. Instead, they continuously learn, evaluate, improve, and respond thoughtfully to changing circumstances. Individuals who cultivate this same mindset become better prepared to recognize new opportunities as the marketplace evolves. **Adaptability allows your value to remain relevant even as the world changes around you.**

As you begin exploring the principles within this chapter, remember that the purpose is not to abandon meaningful work but to expand the way you think about creating value. Whether you are an employee, entrepreneur, investor, educator, author, or professional in any field, you possess opportunities to build knowledge, strengthen systems, develop assets, and serve others more effectively than ever before. **The future belongs not simply to those who work the hardest, but to those who consistently create value that continues working long after today's work has been completed.**

Building Systems That Work Without You

One of the defining differences between traditional work and the 4th-Dimensional Business Model is the shift from completing individual tasks to designing systems that consistently create value. A task is something you perform once. A system is a repeatable process that continues producing reliable results with minimal intervention after it has been thoughtfully developed and refined. **Systems transform effort from something temporary into something that can produce lasting impact.** The more effectively you build systems, the more opportunities you create for your work to continue benefiting others even when your direct attention is focused elsewhere.

Every successful organization, regardless of its size, depends upon systems. Airlines use systems to coordinate flights across the world. Hospitals rely on systems to deliver safe patient care. Manufacturers build systems to maintain consistent quality. Authors develop writing schedules and editing workflows. Publishers establish processes for production and distribution. Investors create systems for research, risk management, and portfolio review. These examples demonstrate an important truth: reliable results are rarely accidental. They emerge from thoughtfully designed processes that can be repeated consistently. **A well-designed system reduces uncertainty while increasing efficiency and reliability.**

Building systems begins with observation. Examine activities you perform repeatedly throughout the week. Which tasks consume unnecessary time because they are approached differently each occasion? Which responsibilities require the same decisions over and over again? Repetition often reveals opportunities for improvement. A standardized checklist, written procedure, digital template, automated reminder, or organized workflow can dramatically reduce the mental effort required to complete recurring responsibilities. Simplifying routine tasks allows more attention to be devoted to creative thinking, strategic planning, and meaningful problem-solving.

Documentation is one of the most overlooked components of system building. Many people carry valuable knowledge entirely in their memory, making it difficult to repeat consistently or share with others. Writing clear procedures, creating templates, recording instructional videos, organizing reference materials, and developing checklists preserve knowledge while improving consistency. Documentation also makes future improvements easier because each process can be reviewed, refined, and updated as circumstances change. **Knowledge that exists only in memory remains limited; knowledge that is documented becomes a resource that can continue creating value over time.**

Technology greatly expands the effectiveness of well-designed systems. Calendar automation, project management software, customer relationship management tools, cloud storage, scheduling applications, accounting programs, artificial intelligence assistants, and workflow automation platforms reduce repetitive administrative work while improving accuracy and organization. Used wisely, these tools support productivity without replacing thoughtful human judgment. The objective is not to automate every decision but to automate routine processes so that your energy remains available for creativity, leadership, learning, and innovation.

Systems also strengthen consistency, which is essential for building trust. Customers appreciate dependable service. Readers expect professional-quality books. Clients value timely communication. Teams perform better when expectations are clear. Consistency rarely happens through good intentions alone; it is usually supported by reliable processes that produce predictable results. Every system you improve strengthens your reputation because people learn they can depend upon the quality of your work. **Trust grows when excellence becomes repeatable rather than occasional.**

Another important advantage of systems is scalability. Without systems, growth often creates confusion because increasing demand requires increasing effort without clear organization. Well-designed systems make it possible to serve more people efficiently while maintaining quality. A standardized onboarding process helps new clients. Organized publishing workflows simplify book production. Educational materials can be updated systematically. Customer questions can be answered through comprehensive knowledge bases. Growth becomes far more sustainable when supported by repeatable structures instead of constant improvisation.

As you continue developing the 4th-Dimensional Business Model, begin asking yourself a new question whenever you complete a recurring task: **"How can I improve this process so it becomes easier, more reliable, and more valuable the next time?"** Small improvements made consistently transform ordinary routines into powerful systems. Over months and years, these systems become invisible assets supporting everything you create. **While individuals accomplish remarkable work, systems allow remarkable work to continue expanding long after the initial effort has been invested.**

Creating Assets That Generate Value Around the Clock

One of the defining characteristics of the 4th-Dimensional Business Model is the intentional creation of assets that continue providing value beyond the hours invested in producing them. Traditional work often ends when the workday ends. An asset, however, has the potential to continue serving people long after its creation. **The objective is not to avoid work but to direct your effort toward building resources that remain useful over time.** Every asset represents stored knowledge, creativity, experience, or problem-solving ability that can continue helping others without requiring you to recreate the same effort repeatedly.

Assets take many different forms, and not all of them are financial investments. A well-written book is an asset because it continues educating readers for years after publication. Educational courses allow expertise to reach students around the world. Software applications solve recurring problems with remarkable efficiency. Digital templates simplify complex tasks for professionals. Research reports organize valuable information into practical guidance. Patents protect innovative inventions. Instructional videos answer common questions repeatedly. Even carefully designed business procedures become assets because they preserve knowledge and improve consistency. **An asset is anything that continues creating value after the original work has been completed.**

Every valuable asset begins with identifying a meaningful need. Rather than asking, "What can I sell?" ask yourself, **"What problem can I solve repeatedly?"** A useful solution often becomes an asset because people continue benefiting from it over time. If customers repeatedly ask the same questions, perhaps the answers belong in a guidebook, online course, or instructional resource. If colleagues struggle with an inefficient process, perhaps a template or software tool could simplify their work. Lasting assets are usually born from careful observation of genuine needs rather than speculation alone.

The creation of enduring assets also requires patience. Few meaningful resources achieve their full value immediately. Authors revise manuscripts numerous times before publication. Entrepreneurs refine products through customer feedback. Developers release software updates that improve functionality. Educators expand courses as industries evolve. Investors allow carefully selected assets time to appreciate responsibly. This gradual refinement is not a sign of failure but evidence of commitment to excellence. **High-quality assets often increase in value because they are continuously improved rather than abandoned after completion.**

Another advantage of asset creation is diversification. A single income source can become vulnerable to unexpected economic changes, industry shifts, or personal circumstances. Building different types of valuable assets creates multiple opportunities to contribute meaningfully while strengthening financial resilience. Someone might combine professional employment with writing books, developing educational resources, investing responsibly, licensing intellectual property, or creating digital tools within their area of expertise. Each asset contributes differently, reducing dependence upon any one source while expanding long-term opportunity.

Technology has made distributing assets more accessible than at any previous point in history. Books can be delivered electronically within seconds. Educational videos reach global audiences. Digital products require no physical inventory. Licensing agreements allow intellectual property to serve multiple organizations simultaneously. Cloud-based software operates continuously regardless of geographical location. These innovations do not guarantee success, but they greatly expand the ability of individuals to share valuable work with people who genuinely need it. **Modern technology allows well-designed assets to continue creating value regardless of time zones or physical distance.**

It is equally important to remember that valuable assets require stewardship. Books benefit from updated editions. Educational materials should reflect current knowledge. Software requires maintenance and security improvements. Businesses evolve with customer needs. Investment portfolios deserve periodic review. Intellectual property should be protected appropriately. Long-term value is strengthened through thoughtful care rather than neglect. The most successful creators recognize that maintaining quality is an ongoing responsibility that preserves trust while extending the useful life of what they have built.

As you continue developing the 4th-Dimensional Business Model, begin evaluating your daily work through a different perspective. Instead of measuring productivity solely by tasks completed today, ask yourself what you are building that will continue serving others tomorrow, next year, or even a decade from now. Every page written, every lesson organized, every process documented, every innovation developed, and every system improved becomes another opportunity to create lasting value. **The greatest wealth often grows from assets that continue helping people long after the original work has ended, allowing today's effort to produce tomorrow's opportunities.**

Thinking Beyond the Limits of Time and Location

One of the greatest advantages of the 4th-Dimensional Business Model is learning to think beyond the traditional limits of time and location. For centuries, most forms of work required people to be physically present in a specific place at a specific time. A merchant had to open a shop, a craftsman worked in a workshop, and a teacher instructed students gathered in a classroom. While these models remain valuable today, technology has dramatically expanded the ways knowledge, products, and services can be shared. **The modern economy rewards those who can create value that reaches people regardless of geography or time zones.**

This shift begins with understanding that your influence is no longer limited to the people living nearby. A book published today can be purchased by readers on multiple continents. An online course can educate students while its creator is asleep. A digital design can be downloaded thousands of times without additional manufacturing. A software application can assist users every hour of every day. A recorded presentation can continue teaching new audiences years after it was first delivered. **Technology allows thoughtfully created value to travel farther than ever before, multiplying its impact without requiring you to be physically present for every interaction.**

Thinking beyond location also encourages broader problem-solving. Rather than designing solutions for only one neighborhood or one community, begin asking whether the challenge exists elsewhere. Many frustrations are universal. People everywhere seek better organization, clearer education, more efficient systems, practical financial guidance, improved health resources, engaging entertainment, and reliable tools that simplify daily life. When your solution addresses a widespread need, its potential impact naturally expands. This does not require serving everyone; it requires serving a clearly defined audience exceptionally well.

Equally important is designing work that remains valuable over time. Some information changes rapidly, while other knowledge remains useful for many years. Educational materials based on timeless principles, practical skills, leadership, communication, creativity, productivity, organization, and thoughtful decision-making often continue helping people long after publication. When creating books, courses, software, or other resources, consider whether the content is likely to remain relevant. **The longer an asset continues providing meaningful value, the greater its long-term contribution to both others and your own financial resilience.**

The 4th-Dimensional Business Model also encourages flexibility in how value is delivered. A single idea may be expressed in multiple formats without changing its core purpose. Research can become a book. A book may inspire workshops. Workshops may evolve into educational videos. Videos may become online courses. Course materials may later develop into templates, guides, or consulting services. Each format serves people with different learning preferences while extending the usefulness of the original work. Rather than constantly searching for entirely new ideas, you can thoughtfully expand the reach of ideas that have already proven valuable.

Another important principle is designing for accessibility. The easier it is for people to discover, understand, and benefit from your work, the greater the likelihood that your value will reach those who need it. Clear writing, organized presentations, intuitive products, straightforward instructions, and thoughtful customer support all improve accessibility. Simplicity should never be confused with lack of depth. Often, presenting complex ideas clearly requires greater mastery than presenting them in complicated ways. **Making valuable knowledge easier to understand increases its usefulness without diminishing its quality.**

Long-term thinking also requires preparing for change. Technologies will continue advancing. Customer expectations will evolve. New industries will emerge while others transform. Individuals who remain committed to learning are better equipped to adapt without abandoning their core mission of creating value. Continuous improvement keeps assets relevant while allowing new opportunities to develop naturally from changing circumstances. Flexibility, curiosity, and thoughtful adaptation become essential qualities within an ever-evolving marketplace.

As you continue developing your own 4th-Dimensional Business Model, remember that your greatest limitations are often not technological but conceptual. Begin asking larger questions. How can your work continue helping people after it is completed? How can your knowledge reach individuals you may never meet personally? How can one idea create value in multiple ways? How can today's effort continue producing benefits years into the future? **When you intentionally think beyond the traditional boundaries of time and location, you begin building work whose influence extends far beyond the hours and places in which it was originally created.**

Designing a Legacy That Outlives Your Lifetime

The highest expression of the 4th-Dimensional Business Model is not measured solely by financial success but by the lasting value your work continues to provide long after it has been completed. Income is important because it creates stability, opportunity, and freedom, but the greatest businesses, books, inventions, educational resources, and organizations are remembered because they improved people's lives in meaningful ways. **A true legacy is built when the value you create continues serving others across generations.** Every system you design, every asset you develop, and every lesson you share becomes part of something larger than yourself.

Many people mistakenly believe that legacy is something created only near the end of life. In reality, legacy begins with today's decisions. Every habit you establish, every project you complete, every person you help, and every problem you solve contributes to the reputation and influence you are building. Whether you realize it or not, your daily actions quietly shape how your work will be remembered. A single thoughtful decision made consistently over many years often has a far greater impact than one extraordinary achievement accomplished in isolation.

Designing a lasting legacy requires creating work that remains valuable regardless of changing trends. While some opportunities are temporary, others are rooted in timeless human needs. People will continue seeking knowledge, practical solutions, thoughtful leadership, creativity, education, organization, effective communication, financial wisdom, and meaningful stories. By focusing on principles that remain useful across different seasons and technological changes, you increase the likelihood that your work will continue helping future generations. **Timeless value often outlasts temporary popularity.**

Legacy is also strengthened through documentation. Knowledge preserved in books, journals, educational materials, research, digital archives, instructional guides, and well-organized systems can continue educating people long after the creator is no longer personally involved.

Every documented lesson reduces the possibility that valuable experience will be forgotten. Throughout history, written knowledge has preserved scientific discoveries, artistic achievements, leadership principles, philosophical ideas, and practical wisdom that continue benefiting society centuries after they were first recorded. Documentation transforms personal experience into a lasting contribution.

Another important element of legacy is developing others. Some of the most influential leaders are remembered not only for what they personally accomplished but for the people they encouraged, mentored, educated, and inspired. Sharing knowledge strengthens communities because it allows wisdom to multiply rather than remain limited to one individual. Teaching others how to think critically, solve problems responsibly, create value ethically, and continue learning ensures that your influence extends beyond your own direct efforts. **The greatest investments often grow through the success of those you help along the way.**

Long-term thinking also encourages responsible stewardship of the resources entrusted to you. Financial assets, intellectual property, businesses, professional relationships, and educational materials all require thoughtful care if they are to continue benefiting others. Regular improvement, careful planning, ethical leadership, and sound decision-making preserve the quality of what you create while preparing it to remain useful for years to come. A lasting legacy is not built through neglect but through consistent attention to excellence and integrity.

The 4th-Dimensional Business Model reminds us that meaningful success is measured not only by what we accumulate but by what we contribute. Wealth becomes more significant when it enables education, innovation, creativity, service, opportunity, and positive influence. Every project becomes an opportunity to leave something better than you found it. Every system improved saves future time. Every book written shares knowledge. Every invention solves a problem. Every ethical business strengthens trust within its community. **When contribution becomes the foundation of your work, financial success often be-**

comes one of many positive outcomes rather than the only objective.

As you complete this chapter, remember that the most enduring businesses are built on principles that extend beyond immediate profit. They solve meaningful problems, adapt thoughtfully to change, develop reliable systems, create lasting assets, and improve the lives of those they serve. Whether your goal is to write books, build a company, develop educational resources, create technology, invest responsibly, or strengthen an existing career, begin asking yourself one final question: **"Will the work I create today continue making someone's life better tomorrow?"** If the answer is yes, you are already building something far more valuable than temporary success—you are designing a legacy capable of creating opportunity, knowledge, and value long after today's work has been completed.

Exercise 1: Design Your 4th-Dimensional Business Model

The purpose of this exercise is to help you begin designing a business or professional model that creates value beyond the hours you personally work each day. The objective is not to leave your current career or immediately launch a company. Instead, this exercise encourages you to identify knowledge, skills, systems, and assets that can continue benefiting others while expanding your long-term opportunities. **Think of this exercise as creating the blueprint for work that continues producing value long after today's effort has been completed.**

Step 1: Identify Your Greatest Strengths

Create a list of at least ten skills, areas of knowledge, hobbies, professional experiences, or personal interests that you possess.

Examples include:

- Writing
- Teaching
- Graphic design
- Photography
- Accounting
- Leadership
- Marketing
- Cooking
- Programming
- Public speaking

Do not judge whether each skill is "good enough."
Simply identify what you already know.

Step 2: Identify Problems You Can Solve

Next to every skill, write at least three problems that knowledge could help solve.

Example:

Writing:

- Help businesses communicate better.
- Teach aspiring authors.
- Create educational books.

Leadership:

- Improve team communication.
- Train new managers.
- Develop leadership resources.

Focus on solving problems rather than selling products.

Step 3: Brainstorm Possible Assets

For every problem you identified, list assets that could provide a solution.

Examples include:

- Books
- Digital guides
- Courses
- Templates
- Checklists
- Videos
- Software
- Membership communities
- Workshops
- Consulting services

Remember that one idea can become many different assets.

Step 4: Evaluate Scalability
Ask yourself the following questions about each asset:

- Can this continue helping people after I create it?
- Can it reach people beyond my local community?
- Can it be improved over time?
- Could many people benefit from it?

Circle the ideas with the greatest long-term potential.

Step 5: Choose One Primary Project

Select only one asset to begin building.

Avoid trying to pursue multiple major projects simultaneously.

Focused attention generally produces higher-quality results than divided attention.

Step 6: Break the Project Into Small Tasks

Create a list of twenty to fifty small actions required to complete your project.

Examples:

- Research the audience.
- Write an outline.
- Choose a title.
- Gather reference materials.
- Draft Chapter One.
- Design the cover.
- Review the manuscript.

Every large accomplishment is completed one manageable step at a time.

Step 7: Schedule Your Daily Progress

Choose one ten-minute period every day dedicated exclusively to your project.

Write it on your calendar.

Protect this appointment exactly as you would any important professional commitment.

Step 8: Build a Simple Workflow
Create a repeatable process.
Example:

- Learn
- Create
- Improve
- Review

Repeat this workflow every day until your project is complete.
Systems create consistency.

Step 9: Identify Helpful Technology

List digital tools that could improve your efficiency.
Examples include:

- Writing software.
- Cloud storage.
- Project management applications.
- Artificial intelligence assistants.
- Graphic design programs.
- Accounting software.
- Calendar automation.

Choose tools that support your work rather than distract from it.

Step 10: Measure Progress Weekly

Every week, answer:

- What did I complete?
- What slowed me down?
- What did I learn?
- What should I improve next week?

Small adjustments prevent large problems later.

Step 11: Imagine the Long-Term Impact

Write a one-page description answering:

- Who will this asset help?
- Why does it matter?
- How could it continue creating value five years from now?
- How might it continue helping people after I complete it?

Think beyond immediate income.
Focus on lasting contribution.

Step 12: Commit to Continuous Improvement

Finish by writing the following commitment:

"I will focus on creating lasting value rather than temporary activity. Every day I will improve my knowledge, strengthen my systems, and build assets that continue serving others long after today's work has ended."

Read this commitment at the beginning of every work session to remind yourself that your goal is not simply to stay busy—it is to create meaningful, enduring value.

Why This Exercise Matters

Many people spend their entire careers completing tasks without ever building assets that continue working on their behalf. This exercise shifts your thinking from short-term productivity to long-term value creation. By identifying your strengths, solving meaningful problems, creating scalable assets, building reliable systems, and improving them consistently, you begin laying the foundation for work that can continue benefiting others for many years. **The most valuable businesses are often built one intentional decision, one thoughtful system, and one carefully developed asset at a time.**

Journal Prompts

1. What does the **4th-Dimensional Business Model** mean to me, and how does it differ from the traditional way I have viewed work?
2. Which of my current skills, knowledge, or life experiences could become an asset that continues helping others long after I create it?
3. If I stopped thinking in terms of hourly income, what kinds of long-term value would I begin building instead?
4. What repetitive tasks in my personal or professional life could be transformed into systems that save time and improve consistency?
5. Which type of asset—books, digital products, educational resources, software, consulting, investments, or something else—best matches my strengths and interests?
6. What habits or routines currently prevent me from thinking beyond today's responsibilities, and how can I replace them with habits that encourage long-term thinking?
7. If I dedicated ten focused minutes every day to building one lasting asset, what could realistically exist one year from now?
8. How can I use technology more intentionally to increase the value, reach, and accessibility of the work I create?
9. What kind of legacy do I want my work to leave for future generations, and what actions can I begin taking today to move toward that vision?
10. Looking back at this chapter, what is the single most important change I will make in the way I think about work, value creation, and building lasting wealth?

Closing Reflection

For generations, success was often measured by the number of hours worked. While dedication, discipline, and honest effort remain essential, the modern world offers an additional opportunity—the ability to create value that continues serving others long after today's work has been completed. This is the heart of the **4th-Dimensional Business Model**. It is not about working less or avoiding responsibility. It is about directing your effort toward building systems, assets, knowledge, and solutions that continue creating meaningful impact over time.

Throughout this chapter, you explored the difference between completing tasks and building assets, between reacting to daily responsibilities and designing systems that improve consistency, and between earning income once and creating resources that continue providing value. You discovered that every book, course, invention, software application, investment, business process, and educational resource begins with one simple decision: to create something that remains useful beyond the present moment.

Remember that **every lasting asset begins as a small daily investment of time, attention, and purpose.** The systems you build today reduce unnecessary effort tomorrow. The knowledge you organize today may educate someone years from now. The business you begin today may continue serving people long after it has matured. The reputation you establish through integrity, excellence, and reliability becomes an invisible asset that opens doors throughout your life.

Do not become discouraged if your first efforts appear modest. Every respected author once wrote a first page. Every successful entrepreneur launched a first project. Every enduring organization began with a simple idea supported by consistent action. Great systems are refined over time. Great assets are improved through experience. Great legacies are built through thousands of thoughtful decisions rather than one dramatic moment.

As you continue your journey through *Quantum Cashflow*, challenge yourself to think beyond today's paycheck and beyond today's workload. Ask yourself regularly:

- **What am I building that will continue creating value next year?**
- **What system can I improve today?**
- **What asset can I develop that will continue helping people long after it is finished?**
- **How can I leave every project better than I found it?**

The answers to those questions will gradually transform the way you approach work, opportunity, and wealth.

When you stop measuring success solely by the hours you work and begin measuring it by the value you create, the systems you build, and the lives you improve, you move beyond simply earning a living—you begin creating a legacy of lasting opportunity, enduring contribution, and sustainable prosperity.

Chapter 5: The Silent Wealth Pipeline—Making Millions Without Public Attention

---

The Quiet Power of Consistent Value Creation

Modern culture often celebrates visibility. Social media highlights viral success stories, headlines focus on overnight entrepreneurs, and public recognition is frequently mistaken for financial achievement. This constant exposure creates the illusion that wealth requires constant attention, a massive audience, or celebrity status. In reality, countless individuals build highly successful businesses, investment portfolios, intellectual property, and professional careers while remaining largely unknown to the general public. **Financial success and public recognition are not the same thing.** One measures attention; the other measures value, stewardship, and long-term contribution.

The phrase **"Silent Wealth Pipeline"** represents a practical approach to creating steady, sustainable financial growth through systems, assets, and consistent value rather than constant public exposure. It does not suggest secrecy or avoiding legitimate business relationships. Instead, it emphasizes that meaningful wealth can be built quietly by solving real problems, serving customers exceptionally well, improving systems continuously, and allowing the quality of your work to become your strongest advertisement. Many thriving businesses operate successfully for decades with little public attention because their reputation spreads through satisfied customers rather than constant publicity.

One of the greatest advantages of building wealth quietly is the freedom to focus on substance instead of appearance. When success becomes dependent upon public approval, valuable time and energy may be diverted toward maintaining an image rather than improving products, strengthening services, or developing new ideas. A silent wealth builder directs attention toward creating genuine value. Every improvement to a product, every enhancement to customer service, every refinement of a business process, and every investment in personal education strengthens the foundation of long-term prosperity. **Quiet progress often produces stronger results than constant self-promotion.**

This principle can be seen throughout many industries. Manufacturers produce components used around the world without becoming household names. Software developers create specialized tools serving thousands of organizations while remaining unknown outside their professional communities. Authors build extensive backlists that continue generating royalties year after year. Engineers design technologies that improve everyday life without receiving public recognition. Investors quietly accumulate assets through disciplined strategies over long periods. These individuals demonstrate that financial success frequently grows through consistency rather than constant visibility. **The marketplace rewards usefulness far more consistently than popularity.**

The Silent Wealth Pipeline also encourages patience. Public attention often rises and falls rapidly, but carefully developed assets continue creating value long after trends have changed. A thoughtfully written reference book may educate readers for decades. Reliable software may support businesses for years through regular updates. Educational resources continue helping students long after their initial publication. Businesses built upon excellent customer relationships frequently grow through referrals instead of expensive advertising. While rapid growth sometimes occurs, sustainable growth is more often the result of persistent improvement repeated over many years. **Patience allows quality to mature into reputation, and reputation becomes one of the strongest drivers of lasting opportunity.**

Another characteristic of silent wealth is intentional privacy. Financial wisdom does not require broadcasting every accomplishment, every investment, or every business decision. Quiet professionals often spend less time comparing themselves to others because their attention remains fixed on their own goals and responsibilities. This perspective reduces unnecessary pressure while encouraging disciplined decision-making based on long-term objectives rather than public perception.

True financial confidence rarely depends upon external validation because it is rooted in thoughtful preparation and consistent execution.

Building a Silent Wealth Pipeline also means allowing your work to speak on your behalf. Exceptional customer service encourages referrals. High-quality books attract loyal readers. Reliable products generate repeat business. Ethical leadership strengthens trust among employees, clients, and partners. Professionalism creates confidence that extends beyond any single transaction. Over time, every satisfied customer, reader, client, or collaborator becomes an ambassador for the value you consistently provide. This steady accumulation of trust often proves more durable than attention generated by temporary publicity. **Reputation compounds in much the same way that investments compound—through consistent positive results over time.**

As you begin this chapter, remember that lasting prosperity is not measured by how many people recognize your name but by how effectively your work improves the lives of others. Whether you build a business, publish books, create educational resources, develop software, invest responsibly, or strengthen an existing career, your greatest advantage will always be the value you consistently deliver. **The Silent Wealth Pipeline is built one thoughtful decision, one meaningful improvement, one satisfied customer, and one valuable asset at a time. While attention may come and go, genuine value continues creating opportunities long after the spotlight has moved elsewhere.**

Building Wealth Through Invisible Assets

One of the greatest misconceptions about wealth is that valuable assets must always be visible. People often notice office buildings, expensive equipment, retail stores, or physical products because they are easy to see. Yet some of the most valuable assets in the modern economy cannot be touched at all. Intellectual property, specialized knowledge, trusted relationships, efficient systems, recognizable brands, copyrights, patents, digital products, software, and professional reputation frequently generate tremendous value while remaining largely invisible. **Invisible assets often become the strongest foundation of long-term financial success because they can continue creating value without requiring constant physical expansion.**

Knowledge is one of the most powerful invisible assets a person can develop. Every book you read, every skill you master, every challenge you overcome, and every lesson you learn becomes part of a growing reservoir of expertise. Unlike many physical possessions, knowledge generally increases in value when it is applied thoughtfully and shared responsibly. An experienced engineer, teacher, physician, designer, author, consultant, or entrepreneur carries years of accumulated learning that can be transformed into solutions benefiting countless others. **The more effectively knowledge solves problems, the more valuable it becomes in the marketplace.**

Reputation is another invisible asset that quietly influences nearly every professional opportunity. Trust cannot be purchased instantly, nor can it be manufactured through advertising alone. It is built through countless interactions in which promises are kept, quality is maintained, communication remains honest, and integrity guides decisions. Customers return because they trust consistency. Employers promote dependable professionals. Readers purchase additional books from authors whose previous work proved valuable. Clients recommend businesses that consistently exceed expectations. Over time, reputation becomes an invisible form of capital that continues opening doors long after the original effort has been forgotten.

Systems also qualify as invisible assets because they improve efficiency without always being noticed. A well-designed publishing workflow, organized financial records, reliable customer support procedures, automated administrative tasks, or carefully documented operating processes all contribute to stronger long-term performance. While customers may never see these systems directly, they experience the results through faster service, higher quality, clearer communication, and greater reliability. **The strongest organizations often succeed because of processes that remain almost entirely invisible to those they serve.**

Relationships represent another extraordinary form of invisible wealth. Genuine professional connections, trusted mentors, collaborative partnerships, loyal customers, and supportive communities create opportunities that cannot easily be measured on a balance sheet. A thoughtful introduction may lead to a lifelong business partnership. A mentor's advice may prevent costly mistakes. Loyal readers may recommend books to friends for years. Clients who receive exceptional service frequently become repeat customers. Every relationship built upon trust, respect, and mutual value strengthens the foundation of sustainable financial growth. Unlike transactional interactions, authentic relationships continue creating opportunities long after individual projects have ended.

The digital economy has dramatically increased the importance of invisible assets. A copyright protects original creative work. A patent safeguards innovation. A recognizable brand builds confidence. A library of educational content continues teaching new audiences. Software code performs valuable work behind the scenes. Search engine visibility quietly introduces customers to businesses every day. Digital infrastructure allows organizations to serve global markets efficiently without requiring extensive physical expansion. **Much of today's economic value exists in information, organization, creativity, and intellectual property rather than in physical inventory alone.**

Protecting invisible assets is just as important as creating them. Knowledge should be updated continuously. Professional reputations require consistent integrity. Customer relationships deserve ongoing care. Intellectual property should be managed responsibly. Business systems benefit from regular refinement. Learning must continue as industries evolve. These assets grow stronger through thoughtful stewardship rather than neglect. The more carefully they are maintained, the more resilient they become during periods of economic change and technological advancement.

As you continue building your Silent Wealth Pipeline, remember that your most valuable resources may never appear on a shelf or inside a warehouse. Your expertise, reputation, relationships, creativity, systems, and intellectual property represent forms of wealth capable of generating value for decades when developed intentionally. Invest in them patiently. Improve them consistently. Protect them wisely. **Invisible assets often produce the most visible results because they quietly strengthen every opportunity, every project, and every meaningful contribution you make throughout your lifetime.**

Creating Multiple Streams of Quiet Cashflow

One of the defining characteristics of a Silent Wealth Pipeline is that it does not rely entirely on a single source of income. While many people begin their financial journey through one primary job or profession, long-term financial resilience often grows by gradually developing additional streams of value over time. This does not mean attempting dozens of unrelated projects simultaneously or working endlessly without rest. Instead, it means thoughtfully building complementary sources of income that support one another while remaining aligned with your knowledge, interests, and long-term goals. **Financial stability is often strengthened when value flows through multiple well-managed channels rather than depending entirely upon one source.**

Multiple streams of cashflow are most effective when they originate from a common foundation of expertise. An educator may teach classes, write books, develop online courses, offer consulting services, and create educational templates. A software developer may build applications, license code, provide technical consulting, and teach programming. An artist may sell original work, license designs, publish instructional guides, and offer workshops. Rather than constantly starting over, each new asset expands upon knowledge that has already been developed. **One area of expertise can often support many different opportunities when organized thoughtfully.**

Building additional streams should occur gradually rather than all at once. Attempting to launch numerous major projects simultaneously often divides attention, reduces quality, and increases unnecessary stress. A more sustainable approach is to strengthen one income-producing asset before beginning another. For example, an author may first establish a catalog of books before creating companion journals or educational resources. A consultant may refine one service before expanding into online training. Each completed project provides experience, confidence, and systems that make future projects more efficient.

Steady expansion generally produces stronger long-term results than rapid, unfocused growth.

One of the greatest advantages of multiple streams is increased resilience during periods of change. Markets fluctuate. Industries evolve. Customer preferences shift. Economic conditions may influence one area while leaving another relatively stable. When income is supported by several complementary sources, temporary challenges affecting one stream do not necessarily interrupt overall financial progress. Diversification does not eliminate risk, but it reduces dependence upon any single opportunity while increasing flexibility and adaptability.

Another important principle is ensuring that each stream continues creating genuine value. Sustainable cashflow is built upon usefulness rather than volume alone. A single well-designed educational course that consistently helps learners may produce greater long-term value than dozens of poorly organized resources. A carefully researched book may remain relevant for years. A reliable software tool may quietly serve businesses every day. Quality attracts trust, and trust encourages repeat customers, referrals, and lasting relationships. **Long-term cashflow grows strongest when every stream is supported by excellence rather than constant expansion alone.**

Technology allows multiple streams of value to operate together more efficiently than ever before. A website introduces readers to books. Books direct readers to educational resources. Courses support consulting services. Newsletters strengthen relationships with customers. Digital payment systems simplify transactions. Automated communication tools improve customer support. Each component strengthens the others, creating an interconnected ecosystem rather than isolated projects. Well-designed systems allow these assets to complement one another while remaining manageable through consistent organization.

Patience remains essential throughout this process. Many people become discouraged because they expect every new project to generate immediate financial results. In reality, lasting cashflow often develops gradually as assets accumulate, reputations strengthen, customer relationships deepen, and systems improve. Every completed book, every satisfied client, every refined process, and every lesson learned contributes to a stronger overall foundation. **Compounding applies not only to investments but also to knowledge, trust, experience, and carefully developed assets.**

As you continue building your Silent Wealth Pipeline, remember that the objective is not to become busy with countless projects but to create a thoughtful collection of valuable assets that work together harmoniously. Each stream should reinforce your mission, strengthen your expertise, and increase the positive impact you have on others. Over time, these interconnected sources of value create a financial structure that is stronger, more adaptable, and less dependent upon any single opportunity. **Quiet, consistent diversification built upon meaningful value often becomes one of the strongest foundations for lasting financial independence.**

The Discipline of Quiet Growth

One of the greatest advantages of building wealth quietly is the ability to remain focused on long-term progress instead of short-term recognition. In a world where achievements are often measured by followers, likes, headlines, and public attention, it can be tempting to mistake visibility for success. Yet many financially successful individuals spend very little time seeking attention because their primary focus remains on improving products, refining systems, strengthening relationships, and consistently serving others. **Quiet growth is often sustainable growth because it is built upon substance rather than constant public validation.**

Discipline is the foundation of this approach. Wealth rarely develops because of one extraordinary decision. More often, it grows through thousands of ordinary choices made consistently over many years. Saving responsibly, investing thoughtfully, improving professional skills, maintaining high standards, honoring commitments, reviewing goals, and continuing to learn may not generate dramatic headlines, but these habits steadily strengthen financial stability. Each disciplined action becomes another brick in the foundation of a resilient financial future. **Consistency quietly accomplishes what occasional bursts of enthusiasm often cannot.**

Another characteristic of quiet growth is resisting unnecessary comparison. Every person's financial journey unfolds under different circumstances, influenced by unique experiences, opportunities, responsibilities, and goals. Constantly comparing your progress with someone else's visible success can lead to discouragement or impulsive decision-making. Instead, compare today's habits with yesterday's habits. Ask whether your knowledge has increased, your systems have improved, your assets have expanded, and your ability to create value has strengthened. **The most meaningful competition is often with the person you were yesterday rather than with someone else today.**

Quiet growth also encourages careful stewardship of resources. Every dollar saved, every investment researched, every business process improved, and every lesson documented contributes to long-term resilience. Financial discipline involves making thoughtful decisions even when no one else notices. Preparing a budget, maintaining emergency reserves, reducing unnecessary expenses, updating professional knowledge, and refining business systems may appear ordinary, yet these actions create extraordinary stability over time. Strong financial foundations are usually built through private discipline rather than public celebration.

Patience becomes increasingly important as wealth compounds. Many valuable assets require months or years before their full potential becomes visible. A book catalog expands gradually. Customer trust develops one interaction at a time. Investment portfolios generally appreciate through long-term discipline rather than constant trading. Business systems improve through continuous refinement. Professional reputations strengthen through years of dependable performance. Individuals committed to quiet growth understand that meaningful progress often occurs beneath the surface long before it becomes visible to others. **Just as trees develop extensive root systems before reaching impressive heights, lasting prosperity often grows invisibly before producing obvious results.**

Another benefit of quiet growth is greater freedom to experiment, learn, and improve without unnecessary external pressure. Not every idea succeeds immediately. New systems require adjustment. Products evolve through customer feedback. Skills improve with practice. When attention remains focused on learning rather than appearances, mistakes become valuable teachers instead of public disappointments. This perspective encourages thoughtful innovation because growth is measured by progress rather than perfection. Every lesson learned strengthens future decision-making.

Quiet growth also supports personal balance. Financial success should complement a meaningful life rather than consume it entirely. Strong relationships, physical health, intellectual curiosity, emotional resilience, ethical leadership, and continued learning all contribute to sustainable prosperity. Wealth becomes far more valuable when it supports a balanced life filled with purpose, service, creativity, and meaningful experiences. **A truly successful financial journey strengthens every important area of life rather than requiring their sacrifice.**

As you continue developing your Silent Wealth Pipeline, remember that the strongest foundations are often built quietly. Continue improving your knowledge. Continue refining your systems. Continue strengthening your reputation. Continue serving others with excellence. Allow your results to grow steadily through disciplined action rather than seeking immediate recognition. Over time, the quiet habits practiced consistently behind the scenes become the visible achievements others admire. **Lasting wealth is rarely built in the spotlight—it is built through years of thoughtful decisions, consistent discipline, and unwavering commitment to creating genuine value.**

Exercise 1: Design Your Silent Wealth Pipeline

The purpose of this exercise is to help you identify, organize, and begin building a personal wealth pipeline that quietly creates long-term value. Rather than depending entirely on one source of income or one major opportunity, this exercise encourages you to develop a thoughtful system of assets, skills, relationships, and consistent habits that strengthen your financial future over time. **The objective is not rapid wealth but sustainable wealth built upon continuous value creation, wise stewardship, and disciplined growth.**

Step 1: Define Your Long-Term Vision

Write a detailed description of what financial success looks like to you ten years from today.

Include questions such as:

- What kind of work am I doing?
- How do I spend my time?
- What assets have I created?
- How do I help other people?
- What does financial freedom allow me to do?

Focus on clarity rather than perfection.

Step 2: List Your Existing Assets

Create a complete inventory of assets you already possess. Include both visible and invisible assets such as:

- Professional skills
- Education
- Certifications
- Books
- Digital products
- Intellectual property
- Business relationships
- Industry knowledge
- Software
- Savings and investments
- Personal reputation

Many people discover they already possess more valuable resources than they realized.

Step 3: Identify Your Strongest Area of Expertise
Choose the area in which you currently provide the greatest value. Ask yourself:

- What do people regularly ask me for help with?
- Which skills have I developed over many years?
- What problems can I solve confidently?

Your greatest expertise often becomes the strongest foundation for additional opportunities.

Step 4: Brainstorm Additional Value Streams
Using your expertise, list every possible way you could create value. Examples include:

- Books
- Courses
- Digital downloads
- Memberships
- Consulting
- Workshops
- Templates
- Licensing
- Educational videos
- Newsletters
- Professional speaking
- Software

Do not evaluate ideas yet.
Simply generate possibilities.

Step 5: Choose Three Long-Term Projects
Select three opportunities with the greatest long-term potential. Ask:

- Will this continue helping people years from now?
- Does it solve a meaningful problem?
- Can I realistically complete it?

Write your reasons for choosing each one.

Step 6: Organize Your Projects by Priority

Place your projects in order.

Project One becomes your immediate focus.

Projects Two and Three remain future priorities.

Avoid dividing your attention between too many major initiatives.

Focused progress produces stronger results.

Step 7: Create a Weekly Progress Schedule
Schedule recurring work sessions.
Example:

- Monday: Research
- Tuesday: Creation
- Wednesday: Improvement
- Thursday: Marketing
- Friday: Review
- Weekend: Reflection and planning

Consistency matters more than intensity.

Step 8: Strengthen One Invisible Asset

Choose one invisible asset to improve this month.
Examples include:

- Professional reputation
- Industry knowledge
- Customer relationships
- Writing ability
- Leadership skills
- Financial literacy
- Communication

Write one practical action you will complete every week.

Step 9: Build a Referral Mindset

Instead of asking,

"How can I attract attention?"

Ask,

"How can I create work so valuable that people naturally recommend it?"

Write five improvements that would make your products or services more helpful.

Step 10: Review Your Pipeline Monthly

At the end of every month, evaluate:

- Which assets grew?
- Which projects moved forward?
- What systems became more efficient?
- Which opportunities appeared unexpectedly?
- What should improve next month?

Small monthly improvements create remarkable long-term results.

Step 11: Measure Value Before Income

Before measuring financial results, answer:

- Did I solve meaningful problems?
- Did I improve quality?
- Did I strengthen trust?
- Did I increase my knowledge?
- Did I help someone today?

Value often precedes financial reward.

Step 12: Write Your Silent Wealth Commitment

Complete the following statement:

"I will build lasting prosperity through consistent value creation, ethical leadership, disciplined learning, thoughtful stewardship, and quiet excellence. My focus will remain on improving my work, serving others well, and strengthening my assets one intentional day at a time."

Read this commitment every week as a reminder that sustainable wealth is built patiently through consistent action rather than temporary attention.

Why This Exercise Matters

The strongest financial foundations are often built quietly, one thoughtful decision at a time. This exercise encourages you to move beyond chasing immediate income and begin constructing a lasting system of knowledge, relationships, assets, and disciplined habits that continue creating value for years to come. As your Silent Wealth Pipeline grows, each improvement strengthens every other part of your financial life. **When value compounds consistently, opportunities often follow naturally, creating prosperity that is resilient, meaningful, and built to endure.**

Journal Prompts

1. What does **The Silent Wealth Pipeline** mean to me, and how does it differ from the way I have traditionally thought about financial success?
2. Which invisible asset—my knowledge, reputation, relationships, systems, or intellectual property—has the greatest potential to create long-term value, and how can I strengthen it?
3. If I stopped seeking recognition and focused entirely on creating exceptional value, how would my daily priorities change?
4. What skills or experiences do I currently possess that could become additional streams of quiet cashflow over the next five years?
5. Which habits consistently strengthen my financial foundation, and which habits quietly weaken my long-term progress?
6. How can I improve my reputation by becoming more reliable, consistent, and valuable in both my personal and professional relationships?
7. Looking at my current projects, which one has the greatest potential to continue serving others long after it is completed?
8. What systems can I build or improve that would allow my work to become more efficient, scalable, and sustainable?
9. If someone described my financial philosophy ten years from now, what qualities would I hope they would mention about my work, integrity, discipline, and contribution?
10. Beginning today, what one quiet action will I take every day to strengthen my Silent Wealth Pipeline and build lasting prosperity without depending on public attention?

Closing Reflection

True wealth rarely announces its arrival with great fanfare. More often, it grows quietly through thousands of thoughtful decisions that few people ever witness. It grows while you continue learning after others have stopped studying. It grows while you improve your products after others have settled for "good enough." It grows while you strengthen relationships, refine systems, protect your reputation, and patiently build assets that continue creating value long after today's work has been completed.

Throughout this chapter, you discovered that **lasting prosperity is not built upon constant visibility but upon consistent usefulness.** Attention may come and go, trends may rise and fall, and public recognition may change with time, but genuine value continues serving people regardless of whether the spotlight is present. Every satisfied customer, every loyal reader, every trusted client, every refined system, every valuable asset, and every ethical decision becomes another part of a financial foundation that quietly grows stronger with each passing year.

Remember that many of the world's most successful individuals are not widely recognized outside their industries. Their wealth was not built by becoming famous—it was built by becoming dependable. They solved meaningful problems, honored their commitments, improved continuously, managed resources wisely, and allowed excellence to become their reputation. **When trust compounds alongside value, opportunity often follows naturally.**

Your greatest financial assets may never appear on a balance sheet. Your knowledge, integrity, creativity, discipline, curiosity, reputation, and relationships influence every opportunity you will ever encounter. Protect them carefully. Invest in them consistently. Improve them deliberately. These invisible forms of wealth often produce the most enduring and meaningful financial results because they strengthen every project you undertake.

As you continue your journey through *Quantum Cashflow*, remember that success does not require constant applause. Some of the strongest trees grow quietly for years before their full height becomes visible. The same is true of lasting wealth. Every book you write, every skill you master, every relationship you nurture, every system you improve, and every problem you solve becomes another branch in a financial structure designed to endure.

Continue building patiently. Continue learning faithfully. Continue serving generously. Continue creating exceptional value with integrity.

The strongest wealth pipelines are built in quiet moments of discipline, strengthened through years of consistent excellence, and sustained by a lifelong commitment to creating value that continues benefiting others long after today's work is done.

Chapter 6: The Reverse Economy Effect—How to Get Paid Before You Do the Work

---

Value First, Delivery Second

For most of modern history, the typical financial exchange has followed a familiar pattern. A person completes work, delivers a product or service, submits an invoice, and eventually receives payment. This sequence has supported countless professions and remains an important part of today's economy. However, many successful businesses operate differently. Customers often pay before a product is manufactured, before a course begins, before a book is released, before a software feature is completed, or before a consulting engagement starts. **The Reverse Economy Effect is not about avoiding work—it is about creating sufficient trust and value that people are willing to invest before final delivery.**

The phrase **"Reverse Economy Effect"** refers to a business model in which value is communicated, demonstrated, and trusted before the completed product or service exists in its final form. This concept should never be confused with making unrealistic promises or collecting payment without intending to deliver. Ethical businesses that receive payment in advance do so because they have clearly explained what customers will receive, established realistic expectations, and built confidence through honesty, professionalism, and previous results. **Trust is the true currency that makes advance payment possible.**

Many familiar industries already operate this way. Conference organizers sell tickets months before the event begins. Airlines receive payment before passengers board the aircraft. Hotels accept reservations before guests arrive. Publishers accept preorders before books are released. Educational institutions receive tuition before classes begin. Subscription businesses collect recurring payments before delivering ongoing services throughout the month. These examples demonstrate that advance payment is not unusual—it is simply supported by systems that inspire confidence. Customers willingly participate because they believe the promised value will be delivered responsibly.

One reason this model works is that customers are rarely purchasing only the finished product. More often, they are purchasing the expected outcome, the solution to a problem, or the experience that product or service will provide. A reader who preorders a book is investing in future knowledge or enjoyment. A student enrolling in a course is investing in future skills. A business hiring a consultant is investing in future improvement. In each case, the purchase reflects confidence in future value rather than immediate possession. **People invest in anticipated benefits when those benefits are communicated clearly and credibly.**

This principle also changes the way creators think about preparation. Instead of waiting until every detail is perfect before sharing an idea, they begin validating whether genuine demand exists. Ethical preorders, pilot programs, limited enrollments, and carefully managed beta releases allow creators to measure interest while gathering valuable feedback before expanding further. These approaches reduce uncertainty because development is guided by actual customer needs rather than assumptions alone. Listening carefully during these early stages often results in stronger products that better serve the people they were designed to help.

However, advance payment creates an even greater responsibility than traditional transactions. Once someone places trust in your promise, your obligation to communicate honestly, meet reasonable timelines, maintain quality, and fulfill commitments becomes even more important. Delays should be explained transparently. Expectations should remain realistic. Challenges should never be hidden behind vague excuses. A reputation built upon dependable delivery strengthens future opportunities, while broken promises quickly damage trust that may have taken years to establish. **Long-term success depends not on receiving payment first, but on consistently exceeding the confidence customers placed in you.**

The Reverse Economy Effect also encourages thoughtful planning. Before offering any preorder, subscription, membership, or advance enrollment, ask yourself important questions. Have I clearly defined what I am delivering? Do I possess the skills and resources necessary to complete this project responsibly? Have I allowed sufficient time for quality work? What risks could delay completion, and how will I communicate if they occur? Careful planning protects both you and your customers while increasing the likelihood of a successful outcome. Responsible preparation is one of the strongest demonstrations of professionalism.

As you begin this chapter, remember that the true lesson is not simply learning how to receive payment before completing work. The deeper lesson is understanding how trust, credibility, preparation, and value creation transform the relationship between creators and customers. **People rarely pay in advance because of persuasive marketing alone—they pay because they believe in the integrity, competence, and reliability of the person creating the value.** When trust becomes the foundation of your work, opportunities naturally expand, relationships strengthen, and sustainable financial growth becomes far more achievable.

Building Trust Before Making the Offer

One of the greatest misunderstandings in business is the belief that customers make purchasing decisions based only on price or features. While both certainly influence decisions, they are rarely the only factors involved. In most situations, people are asking themselves a much deeper question: **"Do I trust this person or organization to deliver what they promise?"** Trust reduces uncertainty. When uncertainty decreases, confidence increases. The Reverse Economy Effect depends upon this principle because people are far more willing to invest before delivery when they believe the creator is reliable, transparent, and committed to providing genuine value.

Trust is rarely built through one impressive moment. Instead, it develops through many consistent interactions over time. Every honest conversation, every deadline met, every thoughtful response to a question, every product delivered as described, and every commitment honored contributes to a growing reputation. Small actions that may seem ordinary today often become the foundation upon which future opportunities are built. **Reputation is accumulated one decision at a time, and every interaction either strengthens or weakens it.**

Transparency is one of the fastest ways to strengthen trust. Customers appreciate clear communication about what they will receive, how long it will take, what limitations exist, and what they should realistically expect. Honest communication creates confidence because it demonstrates respect for the customer's ability to make informed decisions. Exaggerated claims may attract temporary attention, but realistic expectations supported by dependable delivery create lasting relationships. **People generally prefer predictable honesty over impressive promises that cannot be fulfilled.**

Consistency also plays a vital role. A single excellent experience may encourage someone to purchase once, but consistent excellence encourages them to return and recommend your work to others. Whether you are writing books, providing consulting services, developing software, teaching courses, or operating any other type of business, reliability becomes one of your greatest competitive advantages. Delivering quality repeatedly communicates professionalism more effectively than any advertisement. Over time, consistency transforms satisfied customers into loyal supporters.

Another important way to establish trust is by demonstrating expertise before asking for a commitment. Sharing educational articles, useful guides, sample chapters, instructional videos, practical advice, or thoughtful insights allows people to experience the quality of your work firsthand. This approach focuses on providing value before requesting anything in return. As individuals benefit from your knowledge, confidence naturally develops because they have already experienced your ability to solve problems or communicate effectively. **Demonstrated value often builds stronger trust than promises alone.**

Listening carefully is equally important. Businesses that consistently succeed over long periods usually pay close attention to the needs, questions, and concerns of the people they serve. Feedback reveals opportunities for improvement while helping creators refine products before wider release. Customers who feel heard are more likely to remain loyal because they recognize that their experiences contribute to meaningful improvements. Trust deepens when people know their perspectives are respected rather than ignored.

Professionalism reinforces every aspect of credibility. Clear communication, organized processes, respectful interactions, accurate information, and timely responses all contribute to the overall customer experience. Professionalism is not limited to large organizations. Independent creators, authors, consultants, educators, and entrepreneurs can demonstrate exceptional professionalism through thoughtful preparation and dependable follow-through. **Every detail contributes to the impression that customers form about your reliability, whether consciously or unconsciously.**

As you continue developing the Reverse Economy Effect, remember that advance payment is ultimately the result of confidence rather than persuasion. People invest before delivery because they believe your previous actions demonstrate integrity, competence, and genuine concern for the value you provide. Continue strengthening your reputation through consistent excellence, honest communication, careful preparation, and reliable service. **When trust becomes the foundation of every interaction, opportunities naturally expand because confidence is one of the most valuable assets any creator or business can earn.**

Designing Offers People Want Before They Exist

One of the most powerful ideas behind the Reverse Economy Effect is understanding that people rarely purchase a product simply because it exists. Instead, they invest because they believe it will solve a meaningful problem, save time, improve their lives, increase their knowledge, reduce frustration, or help them achieve an important goal. Whether the product is already completed or still in development, the underlying motivation remains the same: **people invest in outcomes, not merely objects.** The clearer the desired outcome becomes, the easier it is for customers to recognize the value of supporting the project before its completion.

Designing an offer that attracts early interest begins with understanding your audience. Every successful product starts by answering questions such as: Who is this designed to help? What challenge are they experiencing? What results are they hoping to achieve? What alternatives have they already tried? The more clearly you understand these questions, the more effectively you can create something that genuinely serves their needs. Rather than asking, *"What do I want to sell?"* begin asking, **"What problem deserves a thoughtful solution?"** This subtle shift places value creation at the center of every business decision.

An effective offer also communicates expectations clearly. Customers appreciate knowing exactly what they are supporting, what features or benefits they can expect, when delivery is anticipated, and how progress will be communicated throughout development. Clarity reduces uncertainty, while uncertainty often delays purchasing decisions. A well-structured description answers important questions before they are asked, helping potential customers feel informed rather than uncertain. **Transparency is one of the strongest forms of customer service because it replaces confusion with confidence.**

Scarcity should always be genuine rather than manufactured. There are legitimate reasons to limit enrollment in a course, offer a restricted number of consulting appointments, or produce a limited beta release while gathering feedback. These limitations exist to maintain quality, provide appropriate support, or carefully manage growth. Artificial scarcity created solely to pressure people into purchasing quickly often weakens trust over time. Ethical business practices encourage thoughtful decisions instead of emotional urgency. **Long-term relationships are strengthened through honesty rather than manipulation.**

Early supporters often provide benefits that extend far beyond financial contributions. They ask thoughtful questions, identify areas for improvement, suggest useful features, and share experiences that help refine the final product. Their perspectives become valuable sources of market research because they represent the very people the product is intended to serve. Listening carefully during these early stages frequently results in stronger products, clearer communication, and higher overall quality. Every constructive conversation becomes another opportunity to improve before wider release.

Another important aspect of designing compelling offers is demonstrating progress consistently. Customers who support projects before completion appreciate regular updates explaining milestones achieved, improvements made, challenges encountered, and expected next steps. Frequent communication reinforces confidence because it shows that meaningful work is continuing behind the scenes. Even when unexpected delays occur, honest progress reports help preserve trust by demonstrating responsibility and professionalism. **People are generally understanding when they are kept informed through respectful, transparent communication.**

Value should always exceed expectation whenever possible. If customers believe they received more than they anticipated, satisfaction naturally increases, encouraging repeat business, referrals, and long-term loyalty. This does not require adding endless features or making unrealistic promises. Instead, it involves delivering exceptional quality, thoughtful attention to detail, clear communication, and dependable fulfillment. Small improvements that enhance the customer experience often leave lasting positive impressions because they demonstrate genuine care rather than minimum compliance.

As you continue applying the Reverse Economy Effect, remember that the strongest offers are built upon understanding, preparation, and service rather than persuasion alone. Invest time in learning what people genuinely need. Communicate your vision with clarity. Set realistic expectations. Deliver consistently with excellence. Continue refining your work through thoughtful feedback. **When your offer is rooted in solving meaningful problems and supported by unwavering integrity, people are far more likely to recognize its value—even before the finished work is complete.**

Creating Predictable Cashflow Through Recurring Value

One of the greatest challenges faced by many individuals and businesses is the uncertainty of inconsistent income. Completing one project often means immediately searching for the next opportunity, creating an ongoing cycle of starting over. While there is nothing inherently wrong with project-based work, it can become exhausting when every month depends entirely upon finding new customers or negotiating new agreements. **The Reverse Economy Effect encourages building recurring value—systems that allow customers to continue benefiting from your work over time while creating more predictable and sustainable cashflow.**

Recurring value begins by asking a simple but powerful question: **"How can I continue helping this person after today's transaction?"** Instead of viewing every sale as the end of a relationship, begin seeing it as the beginning of a long-term opportunity to provide additional education, support, resources, updates, or services. A single purchase can naturally lead to future value when it is built upon genuine usefulness rather than constant selling. Customers appreciate businesses that continue helping them succeed long after the initial transaction has been completed.

Many business models successfully apply this principle. Membership communities provide ongoing education and discussion. Software companies regularly improve their products through updates and new features. Publishers release revised editions of reference materials. Professional organizations offer continuing education. Consultants provide ongoing advisory services after completing initial projects. Subscription-based learning platforms continually expand their libraries with new content. In each example, customers continue receiving meaningful benefits because value is delivered consistently rather than only once. **People are often willing to continue investing when they continue receiving practical, reliable value in return.**

Building recurring value requires thinking beyond individual products and considering the broader journey of the customer. Imagine someone reading your first book. What questions might naturally arise afterward? What additional knowledge would help them continue progressing? Which tools, resources, or educational materials could support their next stage of learning? Designing your work as a connected ecosystem allows each resource to build naturally upon the previous one. Rather than creating isolated products, you create a pathway of continued growth that benefits both your audience and your long-term business.

Consistency becomes especially important in recurring business models. Customers expect regular communication, dependable updates, accurate information, and ongoing improvement. Delivering value sporadically weakens confidence, while consistent quality strengthens loyalty. This does not mean producing endless amounts of content or constantly introducing new products. Instead, it means maintaining a reliable standard of excellence that customers can confidently expect every time they interact with your work. **Consistency transforms occasional buyers into long-term supporters because reliability builds lasting trust.**

Listening to existing customers also becomes increasingly valuable. Individuals who continue supporting your work often provide the clearest insight into future opportunities. They reveal which resources they found most helpful, what challenges remain unresolved, and what additional solutions would genuinely improve their experience. Rather than guessing what people might need next, thoughtful creators ask, observe, and learn directly from those they already serve. This ongoing dialogue helps ensure that future products remain practical, relevant, and valuable.

Another advantage of recurring value is improved planning. More predictable cashflow allows businesses and independent creators to invest more confidently in better tools, additional education, product improvements, research, customer support, and long-term projects. Instead of constantly reacting to uncertainty, greater stability creates opportunities for thoughtful growth. This financial predictability also reduces unnecessary stress, allowing more attention to remain focused on innovation, quality, and service rather than immediate survival.

As you continue developing the Reverse Economy Effect, remember that the strongest businesses rarely depend upon convincing new customers every day. Instead, they earn continued confidence by consistently creating value that people genuinely appreciate over time. Build relationships rather than transactions. Solve ongoing problems rather than temporary ones. Continue improving what you create instead of constantly replacing it. **When customers recognize that your commitment extends beyond the initial sale, recurring trust naturally becomes recurring opportunity, and recurring opportunity becomes one of the strongest foundations for lasting financial success.**

The Responsibility That Comes With Advance Trust

Receiving payment before completing work is not merely a financial advantage—it is a profound responsibility. Every preorder, subscription, membership, reservation, enrollment, deposit, or advance payment represents something much more valuable than money. It represents confidence. Someone has chosen to trust your integrity, your competence, your planning, and your commitment to delivering what you promised. **The Reverse Economy Effect succeeds only when that trust is treated as a responsibility rather than an entitlement.**

Trust is remarkably difficult to build and surprisingly easy to lose. It develops through repeated experiences in which expectations are met or exceeded, communication remains honest, and commitments are honored consistently. A single broken promise may not permanently damage a relationship if handled transparently and responsibly, but repeated disappointments gradually erode confidence. Individuals and businesses that enjoy lasting success recognize that protecting trust is often more valuable than maximizing short-term profit. **Reputation compounds slowly but can decline quickly when integrity is neglected.**

Preparation is one of the strongest demonstrations of respect for advance trust. Before accepting payment, ensure that you have thoughtfully considered the scope of the project, realistic timelines, available resources, potential challenges, and contingency plans. Responsible planning reduces unnecessary delays while increasing confidence that the final product or service will meet the promised standard. Unexpected difficulties may still arise, but careful preparation significantly improves your ability to respond effectively rather than react impulsively.

Communication becomes even more important after advance payment has been received. Customers should never feel uncertain about the status of a project simply because payment has already been collected. Regular updates, clear explanations of milestones achieved, honest discussions of unexpected challenges, and realistic delivery estimates demonstrate professionalism and respect. Even when progress occurs behind the scenes, thoughtful communication reassures customers that meaningful work continues steadily. **Silence often creates unnecessary uncertainty, while honest communication strengthens confidence even during difficult periods.**

Quality must always remain the priority. There can be a temptation to rush completion simply because payment has already been received, but lasting success depends upon delivering work worthy of the trust customers have placed in you. Whether writing a book, developing software, creating educational materials, consulting, or launching a new product, excellence should remain the objective from beginning to end. Customers who receive exceptional value become long-term supporters because their confidence has been rewarded rather than merely acknowledged.

Accountability is another essential characteristic of ethical leadership. Mistakes occasionally occur in every profession. Deadlines sometimes require adjustment. Features may need refinement. Circumstances beyond anyone's control can influence schedules. Accountability does not require perfection—it requires responsibility. Acknowledge challenges honestly, explain the plan moving forward, and continue working diligently toward fulfillment. Customers generally appreciate sincerity far more than excuses because accountability demonstrates respect for the relationship built through trust.

The Reverse Economy Effect also encourages humility. Receiving advance support is not evidence that you have nothing left to learn. On the contrary, every customer interaction provides an opportunity to improve communication, refine products, strengthen systems, and increase future value. Individuals and organizations committed to continuous improvement view customer feedback as a valuable resource rather than criticism. Each project becomes another opportunity to strengthen both the product and the trust supporting it. **Humility allows ex-**

cellence to continue growing long after initial success has been achieved.

As you conclude this chapter, remember that the Reverse Economy Effect is ultimately about stewardship rather than speed. Advance payment is made possible by trust, and trust is sustained through integrity, preparation, transparency, consistent quality, and genuine concern for those you serve. Financial success achieved without trust rarely endures, but success built upon dependable value often strengthens year after year. **When you consistently honor the confidence others place in your work, you build something far greater than immediate income—you build a reputation capable of creating opportunities for decades to come.**

Exercise 1: Design Your Ethical Advance-Value Business Model

The purpose of this exercise is to help you build a business model that earns trust before requesting payment and delivers exceptional value afterward. The goal is not simply to receive payment earlier—it is to create a professional system where customers feel confident investing in your work because of your preparation, integrity, communication, and proven ability to solve meaningful problems. **A sustainable Reverse Economy Effect begins with earning confidence before asking for commitment.**

Step 1: Define the Problem You Solve

Write a clear description of one meaningful problem your product, service, or expertise helps solve.

Ask yourself:

- Who experiences this problem?
- Why does it matter?
- How does it affect their daily life or work?
- What outcome are they hoping to achieve?

The clearer the problem, the easier it becomes to communicate your value.

Step 2: Describe Your Solution

Write a one-page explanation of your proposed solution. Include:

- What you are creating.
- How it helps.
- Why it is different.
- What practical benefits customers will receive.

Focus on clarity rather than marketing language.

Step 3: Identify Your Ideal Customer
Describe the people who would benefit most from your work. Consider:

- Experience level.
- Goals.
- Challenges.
- Interests.
- Professional background.
- Common questions.

Understanding your audience allows you to communicate more effectively.

Step 4: Build Trust Before Asking for Payment

List at least ten ways you can demonstrate credibility before offering an advance purchase.

Examples include:

- Publishing educational articles.
- Sharing sample chapters.
- Creating instructional videos.
- Providing useful guides.
- Answering common questions.
- Demonstrating previous work.
- Showing testimonials (when appropriate).
- Explaining your process.
- Maintaining professional communication.
- Being transparent about timelines.

Trust should always precede the transaction.

Step 5: Define Exactly What Customers Will Receive
Create a detailed checklist describing your deliverable. Include:

- Features.
- Format.
- Expected completion date.
- Updates customers will receive.
- Any limitations or exclusions.

Clear expectations reduce misunderstandings.

Step 6: Create a Realistic Timeline
Break your project into milestones.
Example:

- Research completed.
- Outline completed.
- First draft finished.
- Editing completed.
- Final review.
- Delivery.

Assign realistic dates to each milestone.
Always leave room for unexpected challenges.

Step 7: Plan Your Communication Schedule
Decide how often you will update customers.
Examples include:

- Weekly updates.
- Biweekly progress reports.
- Monthly newsletters.
- Milestone announcements.

Write exactly what information you will provide during each update. Consistent communication strengthens confidence.

Step 8: Prepare for Unexpected Delays

List potential obstacles that could affect your timeline.

Examples include:

- Technical issues.
- Illness.
- Supply delays.
- Research taking longer than expected.
- Software problems.

Next to each obstacle, write how you will communicate with customers if it occurs.

Preparation protects trust.

Step 9: Define Your Quality Standards

Write the minimum standards every completed project must meet before delivery.

Examples include:

- Proofread carefully.
- Fully tested.
- Accurate information.
- Professional formatting.
- Complete documentation.
- Final quality review.

Never sacrifice quality simply to finish quickly.

Step 10: Plan How You Will Exceed Expectations

Write five small ways you can provide additional value. Examples include:

- Bonus resources.
- Helpful checklists.
- Additional tutorials.
- Frequently asked questions.
- Downloadable templates.
- Follow-up support.

Thoughtful extras often create lasting loyalty.

Step 11: Review Your Entire Customer Experience
Imagine becoming your own customer.
Ask yourself:

- Would I clearly understand the offer?
- Would I feel confident purchasing?
- Would communication feel professional?
- Would delivery meet my expectations?
- Would I recommend this experience to someone else?

Write improvements based upon your answers.

Step 12: Write Your Trust Commitment

Complete the following statement:

"Every opportunity I receive is built upon someone else's confidence in my integrity. I will communicate honestly, prepare carefully, deliver exceptional value, honor every reasonable commitment, and continually improve the quality of my work. My reputation will always be more valuable than any single transaction."

Read this commitment before launching every new project, accepting every preorder, or inviting customers to invest in your work.

Why This Exercise Matters

Advance payment is not simply a financial strategy—it is a reflection of earned confidence. By learning to communicate clearly, plan responsibly, set realistic expectations, maintain consistent communication, and deliver work that exceeds expectations, you create relationships built upon trust rather than persuasion. Over time, this approach strengthens your reputation, encourages repeat customers, generates referrals, and creates a business that is respected because it consistently delivers what it promises. **When trust becomes your greatest asset, sustainable opportunity naturally follows.**

Journal Prompts

1. What does the **Reverse Economy Effect** mean to me, and how has this chapter changed my understanding of how value is exchanged in today's economy?
2. Which products, services, or areas of expertise could I confidently offer through an ethical advance-payment model, and why?
3. What actions can I take today to strengthen my reputation so that people naturally develop greater trust in my work?
4. How can I communicate my ideas more clearly so potential customers fully understand the value I intend to provide?
5. Which professional habits consistently build trust, and which habits could unintentionally weaken my credibility?
6. What systems can I create to ensure every customer receives consistent communication, exceptional quality, and dependable service?
7. Looking at my current projects, which one has the greatest potential to benefit from preorders, memberships, subscriptions, deposits, or another ethical advance-payment model?
8. If I were my own customer, what improvements would make me feel even more confident investing in my work before it is completed?
9. What does long-term trust mean to me, and how can I protect it through honesty, preparation, professionalism, and continuous improvement?
10. Beginning today, what one action will I take to become the type of creator, professional, or business owner that people confidently support because they trust my integrity and the value I consistently deliver?

Closing Reflection

The Reverse Economy Effect is not truly about receiving payment before completing work. It is about earning something far more valuable first—**trust**. Every advance purchase, preorder, subscription, reservation, membership, or deposit represents a decision made by someone who believes in your integrity, your preparation, your professionalism, and your commitment to delivering meaningful value. That confidence is never owed; it is earned through consistent actions and protected through responsible stewardship.

Throughout this chapter, you discovered that people rarely invest in unfinished work because of persuasive marketing alone. They invest because they believe the creator understands their needs, communicates honestly, sets realistic expectations, and has demonstrated the ability to deliver on those promises. Trust reduces uncertainty. Clear communication strengthens confidence. Dependable execution transforms first-time customers into long-term supporters. **When integrity becomes the foundation of your work, financial opportunities often expand naturally because confidence grows with every promise you keep.**

You also learned that advance payment carries significant responsibility. Every customer who chooses to support your work before completion deserves transparency, professionalism, regular communication, realistic timelines, and exceptional quality. The objective is never simply to complete a transaction—it is to build a lasting relationship based upon mutual respect and consistent value. Businesses that thrive over decades are rarely remembered because they collected payment early; they are remembered because they consistently honored the confidence others placed in them.

As your experience grows, remember that your reputation becomes one of your greatest business assets. Every project completed with excellence strengthens it. Every honest conversation reinforces it. Every thoughtful improvement expands it. Every customer treated with respect contributes to it. Unlike advertising, reputation compounds quietly through years of dependable performance and ethical leadership. **Protect your reputation with the same care you would protect your most valuable financial investment, because it influences every future opportunity you will ever receive.**

As you continue through *Quantum Cashflow*, carry this principle with you: people do not simply invest in products—they invest in people they believe will create meaningful value. Continue developing your expertise. Continue strengthening your systems. Continue communicating with honesty. Continue delivering work that reflects your highest standards. Build relationships before transactions, trust before revenue, and value before profit.

When you consistently place integrity before income, service before self-promotion, and lasting trust before short-term gain, you create a business foundation capable of supporting opportunities for years—even decades—to come. In the modern economy, trust is not merely part of success; it is the quiet force that makes sustainable success possible.

Chapter 7: Quantum Branding—Positioning Yourself as a Perceived Billionaire

----

Building a Reputation That Reflects Excellence

A strong personal brand is not built by convincing people you possess extraordinary wealth. It is built by consistently demonstrating professionalism, competence, reliability, and a commitment to creating meaningful value. The phrase **"Positioning Yourself as a Perceived Billionaire"** is used in this chapter as a metaphor for developing the mindset, standards, and reputation often associated with highly successful individuals. It does **not** mean pretending to have financial resources, accomplishments, or credentials that you do not possess. Authenticity remains the foundation of every lasting brand. **The most valuable personal brand is one that truthfully reflects who you are while clearly communicating the value you bring to others.**

Every interaction contributes to your brand, whether you realize it or not. The emails you send, the books you publish, the conversations you have, the promises you keep, the quality of your work, and the way you respond to challenges all shape how people perceive your professionalism. Many people think branding begins with a logo, a website, or a business card. While these visual elements certainly matter, they are only outward expressions of something much deeper. Your reputation is built through repeated experiences in which people discover that your actions consistently match your words. **Branding is not primarily about appearance—it is about earned perception created through consistent behavior.**

People naturally form impressions based on patterns rather than isolated events. One exceptional project may attract attention, but consistent excellence builds confidence. When readers repeatedly enjoy your books, they become more likely to purchase future releases. When clients receive dependable service, they return with additional opportunities. When colleagues recognize your professionalism, they recommend you to others. Over time, each positive experience strengthens your reputation, creating a cycle in which trust generates additional opportunities. **Consistency transforms good work into a recognizable professional identity.**

Professional branding also begins with clarity. Before others can understand the value you provide, you must understand it yourself. Ask yourself what problems you solve, which audiences you serve, what principles guide your work, and what qualities you want people to associate with your name. Perhaps you want to become known for thoughtful leadership, practical education, dependable service, innovative thinking, exceptional writing, or ethical business practices. Clear answers to these questions create direction because every future decision can be evaluated according to whether it strengthens or weakens your desired reputation.

One of the strongest characteristics of respected professionals is attention to detail. Small details often communicate larger messages about quality and care. Clear writing, organized presentations, accurate information, professional formatting, thoughtful customer communication, and dependable follow-through all contribute to a stronger brand. None of these actions require enormous financial investment. Instead, they require intentional effort and respect for the people you serve. **Excellence is often communicated through small details repeated consistently rather than dramatic gestures performed occasionally.**

Another important aspect of Quantum Branding is emotional consistency. Individuals who remain calm under pressure, communicate respectfully during disagreements, acknowledge mistakes honestly, and respond thoughtfully to unexpected challenges often earn greater long-term trust than those who appear impressive only when circumstances are favorable. Character becomes visible during moments of difficulty. Every challenge presents an opportunity to reinforce your reputation through integrity, professionalism, and responsible leadership. The way you handle adversity often influences your brand as much as the work you produce.

Your brand should also reflect continuous growth. Markets evolve, technologies advance, industries change, and customer expectations develop over time. A respected professional does not remain static. They continue learning, improving, refining their skills, and expanding their knowledge. This commitment to lifelong development strengthens credibility because people recognize that your expertise is supported by ongoing education rather than past accomplishments alone. **A strong brand is not frozen in time—it grows stronger because its owner never stops improving.**

As you begin this chapter, remember that the goal is not to appear wealthy, powerful, or important for the sake of appearances. The true objective of Quantum Branding is to develop a reputation that naturally inspires confidence because it is built upon honesty, excellence, competence, reliability, and meaningful contribution. **When your name consistently becomes associated with quality, integrity, and dependable value, you create a personal brand whose influence extends far beyond marketing. That kind of reputation becomes one of the most valuable assets you will ever build.**

Communicating Value Before You Say a Word

One of the strongest personal brands is one that begins communicating professionalism before a conversation even starts. Long before someone reads your book, hires your services, visits your website, or attends one of your presentations, they begin forming impressions through countless subtle details. The quality of your written communication, the organization of your work, the consistency of your visual identity, the clarity of your message, and the professionalism of your interactions all contribute to those first impressions. **People often develop expectations within moments, but those expectations are usually shaped by patterns of quality rather than by dramatic displays.**

Your communication should always begin with clarity. Confusing language creates uncertainty, while clear language creates confidence. Whether writing a book description, responding to an email, introducing yourself professionally, or explaining a product, your audience should quickly understand what you offer, who it helps, and why it matters. Clarity demonstrates respect because it saves people time and allows them to make informed decisions. **The clearer your message, the easier it becomes for others to recognize the value you provide.**

Consistency is equally important. A strong professional identity communicates the same core values across every interaction. Your books, website, presentations, newsletters, customer service, and conversations should all reflect the same commitment to quality, integrity, and thoughtful service. This does not mean becoming repetitive or rigid. Rather, it means ensuring that your values remain recognizable regardless of the format through which people encounter your work. Consistency strengthens trust because people know what they can reasonably expect whenever they interact with you.

Visual presentation also influences perception, although it should always support substance rather than replace it. Organized documents, professional formatting, readable typography, thoughtful design, and high-quality images communicate care and attention to detail. These elements do not guarantee excellent content, but they encourage confidence that similar care has been invested throughout the work. Every visual decision should reinforce the experience you want others to have rather than distract from the value you are providing. **Professional presentation quietly communicates respect for both your work and your audience.**

Another important aspect of communication is listening. Strong brands are built not only by speaking effectively but also by understanding the needs of the people they serve. Customers, readers, clients, and colleagues often reveal valuable insights through their questions, suggestions, and feedback. Careful listening allows you to improve your work continuously while demonstrating genuine interest in helping others succeed. Individuals who feel heard are far more likely to develop long-term trust because they recognize that their experiences contribute to meaningful improvement.

Your actions must consistently support your message. It is easy to describe yourself as dependable, knowledgeable, or customer-focused, but lasting credibility develops when those qualities are repeatedly demonstrated through real behavior. Meeting deadlines, honoring commitments, providing accurate information, responding respectfully, and maintaining high standards reinforce every statement you make about your professional identity. **Actions remain the strongest form of communication because they provide evidence rather than promises.**

Another characteristic of exceptional communicators is simplicity. Many people assume expertise requires complicated language or impressive terminology. In reality, true expertise often allows complex ideas to be explained clearly and understandably. Whether writing, teaching, consulting, or leading, strive to make valuable information accessible without sacrificing accuracy. Simplicity expands your ability to help others because understanding becomes easier. Clear communication is not a sign of shallow thinking—it is often evidence of deep understanding.

As you continue developing your Quantum Brand, remember that your reputation is constantly being shaped through both visible and invisible communication. Every email sent, every page written, every conversation held, every product delivered, and every promise fulfilled contributes to the story people associate with your name. Rather than asking, **"How can I appear successful?"** begin asking, **"How can every interaction communicate excellence, integrity, clarity, and genuine value?"** When your communication consistently reflects these qualities, your personal brand becomes a natural extension of your character, allowing trust and opportunity to grow together over time.

Developing an Identity People Instinctively Trust

One of the most valuable qualities of a powerful personal brand is trust. Long before people evaluate your products, services, books, or ideas in detail, they often ask themselves a simple question: **"Can I rely on this person?"** Trust is not created through persuasive language alone. It grows through repeated experiences in which integrity, competence, consistency, and professionalism become evident. The strongest brands are remembered not because they demand attention but because they continually earn confidence through dependable actions.

Developing a trustworthy identity begins with keeping promises—especially the small ones. Responding when you say you will, meeting reasonable deadlines, delivering the quality you described, and communicating honestly when circumstances change all reinforce reliability. Many people focus on making impressive promises while overlooking the importance of fulfilling ordinary commitments. Yet it is often the consistent completion of small responsibilities that creates confidence strong enough to support much larger opportunities. **Reliability demonstrated repeatedly becomes one of the strongest forms of professional credibility.**

Authenticity also plays a vital role in building trust. Attempting to imitate another person's personality, accomplishments, or communication style rarely creates lasting confidence because inconsistency eventually becomes noticeable. Instead, allow your genuine strengths, experiences, values, and expertise to shape the way you present yourself professionally. Authenticity does not mean sharing every personal detail; it means ensuring that your public image accurately reflects your real character and abilities. **A truthful reputation is always more sustainable than an impressive illusion.**

Competence strengthens every aspect of your identity. Individuals naturally trust professionals who clearly understand their field and continue expanding their knowledge. Reading current research, improving technical skills, practicing communication, refining your craft, and staying informed about developments within your profession all contribute to stronger credibility. Expertise should never become an excuse for arrogance; rather, it should encourage humility because every field continues evolving. Lifelong learning demonstrates respect both for your profession and for the people who depend upon your work.

Another important element of trust is consistency under changing circumstances. It is relatively easy to remain professional when everything proceeds according to plan. Greater character is revealed when unexpected challenges arise. Responding calmly, communicating honestly, accepting responsibility when appropriate, and focusing on constructive solutions reinforce confidence because people recognize that your values remain stable even during difficult situations. **Character is most visible when circumstances become challenging, and those moments often influence your reputation more than periods of success.**

Respect for others also strengthens personal identity. Every interaction offers an opportunity to demonstrate professionalism through courtesy, patience, careful listening, and thoughtful communication. Customers appreciate being treated with dignity. Readers value honest engagement. Colleagues remember respectful collaboration. Professional relationships grow stronger when people consistently feel heard, appreciated, and valued. Respect creates an environment where trust naturally develops because individuals recognize that they are more than transactions or statistics.

A trusted identity is further strengthened by continuous improvement. The most respected professionals rarely assume they have reached their final level of development. They seek constructive feedback, evaluate their performance honestly, update their knowledge, improve their systems, and refine the quality of their work. This willingness to improve demonstrates confidence rather than insecurity because it reflects a commitment to excellence instead of perfection. **People place greater trust in individuals who continue growing than in those who believe they have nothing left to learn.**

As you continue building your Quantum Brand, remember that trust cannot be manufactured quickly, purchased directly, or maintained through appearance alone. It is built gradually through truthful communication, dependable actions, consistent quality, ethical decision-making, and genuine concern for those you serve. Every promise honored strengthens your reputation. Every lesson learned improves your competence. Every thoughtful interaction reinforces your character. **When people instinctively associate your name with integrity, reliability, and meaningful value, your personal brand becomes far more powerful than any marketing campaign because it is supported by the strongest foundation possible—earned trust.**

Creating an Ecosystem Instead of a Single Product

One of the defining characteristics of exceptional brands is that they rarely depend upon a single product, service, or opportunity. Instead, they create an interconnected ecosystem in which every resource strengthens the others. Rather than asking, **"How can I sell one product?"** successful creators ask, **"How can I build a collection of valuable resources that help people continue progressing?"** This shift transforms isolated offerings into a complete experience that serves customers over a much longer period of time while strengthening the overall reputation of the brand.

An ecosystem begins with a clear mission. Every book, article, course, presentation, digital product, consultation, or service should contribute to a larger purpose. For example, an educator may focus on helping people develop practical financial skills. Every new resource expands upon that central mission instead of competing with previous work. Readers who benefit from one book naturally discover additional resources that continue supporting their learning. This approach creates continuity because every product feels like another chapter in the same ongoing conversation rather than an unrelated project.

Each part of the ecosystem should solve a different stage of the customer's journey. Someone encountering your work for the first time may need introductory guidance, while others seek advanced strategies or specialized knowledge. Beginners appreciate clear foundations. Experienced individuals often look for deeper insights, practical applications, or advanced techniques. By creating resources for different stages of growth, you remain valuable throughout a customer's continued development rather than serving only a single moment. **A strong brand grows alongside the people it serves.**

Consistency becomes especially important when building an ecosystem. Your books, website, newsletters, educational materials, presentations, customer support, and professional communication should all reflect the same standards of quality and the same commitment to helping others succeed. This consistency strengthens recognition because people immediately understand what your brand represents. Every interaction reinforces the values you want associated with your name, making future resources easier for people to trust.

Thoughtful organization also improves the customer experience. Resources should naturally connect with one another without creating confusion. A foundational book might introduce concepts explored more deeply in a companion workbook, educational course, or consulting service. Articles may answer common questions while directing readers toward additional learning opportunities. Templates may simplify practical implementation. Rather than overwhelming people with unrelated options, each resource should help them identify the logical next step in their journey. **Clear pathways encourage confidence because people know where to go next when they are ready to continue learning.**

An ecosystem also encourages continuous improvement instead of constant replacement. Existing resources can be updated with new research, improved examples, clearer explanations, and better organization. Customer feedback often reveals opportunities to refine current materials before creating entirely new ones. This commitment to improvement demonstrates respect for both your audience and your own work. Over time, the quality of the entire ecosystem increases because each part benefits from lessons learned through previous projects.

Another important advantage is resilience. When your professional identity depends entirely upon one product or one service, unexpected market changes can create unnecessary vulnerability. An ecosystem distributes value across multiple complementary resources, allowing different parts to support one another during changing circumstances. Books continue introducing readers to courses. Courses encourage consulting opportunities. Articles strengthen newsletters. Educational resources build community. Each component contributes to the strength of the whole rather than existing independently.

As you continue developing your Quantum Brand, begin thinking beyond individual projects and toward the larger experience you want people to have whenever they interact with your work. Ask yourself how each new resource strengthens the overall mission, serves your audience more effectively, and contributes to a lasting reputation for excellence. **The strongest brands are rarely remembered for one successful product alone—they are remembered because every part of their work consistently reflects the same commitment to quality, integrity, thoughtful service, and meaningful value.**

Leading With Value Instead of Status

Many people mistakenly believe that powerful branding requires appearing more successful, more influential, or more important than everyone else. They focus on symbols of status while overlooking the qualities that actually create long-term respect. Genuine professional influence is not built by convincing people that you are extraordinary—it is built by consistently demonstrating that you are capable, dependable, ethical, and committed to helping others succeed. **The strongest brands earn admiration through contribution rather than through appearances.**

Status is often temporary because it depends upon external recognition. Value, however, has the potential to endure because it is rooted in usefulness. A bestselling book eventually fades from the bestseller list, but the knowledge within it may continue helping readers for decades. A successful business may experience changing market conditions, yet its commitment to excellent customer service can preserve customer loyalty through difficult seasons. A respected professional may never become famous, but years of dependable work create a reputation that continues opening doors. **Recognition may attract attention, but value sustains opportunity.**

People naturally remember those who improve their lives. An educator who explains difficult concepts clearly, a consultant who solves expensive problems, an author whose books inspire practical action, or a business owner who consistently exceeds expectations all become memorable because of the positive impact they create. Instead of asking, **"How can I appear more successful?"**, begin asking, **"How can I become more useful?"** That single question redirects your attention away from image and toward lasting contribution.

Humility strengthens a professional brand far more than arrogance. Confident individuals acknowledge both their expertise and their willingness to continue learning. They listen carefully before offering advice. They welcome thoughtful feedback because improvement matters more than appearing perfect. They freely recognize the contributions of others instead of attempting to claim every success for themselves. Humility does not diminish authority; it strengthens credibility because people recognize sincerity rather than insecurity. **True confidence is comfortable admitting there is always more to learn.**

Service should become the guiding principle behind every professional decision. Before launching a new book, product, course, presentation, or business initiative, ask yourself whether it genuinely improves the lives of the people it is intended to serve. Will it save them time? Increase their understanding? Reduce frustration? Help them make wiser decisions? Simplify a difficult process? Every meaningful solution strengthens your reputation because customers remember how your work made them feel and what it enabled them to accomplish.

Long-term brands are also built through generosity with knowledge. Sharing practical insights, answering thoughtful questions, publishing educational articles, speaking honestly about lessons learned, and encouraging others to grow all contribute to a reputation for leadership. Providing useful information does not diminish your professional value. In many cases, it increases confidence because people experience your expertise before making larger commitments. **Knowledge shared with integrity often becomes one of the strongest forms of marketing because it demonstrates value rather than merely describing it.**

Ethical decision-making remains essential at every stage of professional growth. Opportunities sometimes arise that promise immediate financial gain while conflicting with your values or long-term reputation. Strong brands recognize that every decision contributes to public perception. Declining opportunities that compromise quality, honesty, or professionalism protects something far more valuable than short-term profit: enduring trust. Reputation grows stronger when principles remain consistent regardless of changing circumstances.

As you continue developing your Quantum Brand, remember that lasting influence is rarely created through prestige alone. It is built through years of thoughtful service, dependable work, ethical leadership, continuous improvement, and genuine concern for the people you serve. Allow your reputation to grow because your work consistently solves meaningful problems rather than because it attracts temporary attention. **When value becomes the foundation of your professional identity, your brand develops a quiet strength that continues creating opportunity long after trends, titles, and public recognition have changed.**

Exercise 1: Design Your Quantum Brand Identity

The purpose of this exercise is to help you intentionally develop a personal or professional brand that reflects your authentic strengths, communicates your values clearly, and consistently builds trust over time. The objective is not to create an artificial image or impress others with appearances. Instead, you will design a brand that accurately represents the quality of your work, the problems you solve, and the positive impact you want to have on the people you serve. **A lasting brand is built through clarity, consistency, integrity, and meaningful value—not through image alone.**

Step 1: Define Your Core Mission
Write one sentence that clearly explains why your work exists.
Ask yourself:

- Who do I want to help?
- What problems do I solve?
- Why does this work matter?
- What positive change do I hope to create?

Keep your mission simple, memorable, and focused on service.

Step 2: Identify Your Core Values
List five to ten values that will guide every decision you make. Examples include:

- Integrity
- Excellence
- Curiosity
- Reliability
- Innovation
- Education
- Compassion
- Professionalism
- Creativity
- Continuous learning

These values should influence your communication, products, customer service, and leadership.

Step 3: Define Your Brand Personality
Describe how you want people to experience your work.
Choose words that genuinely reflect your professional identity.
Examples include:

- Knowledgeable
- Encouraging
- Practical
- Thoughtful
- Organized
- Innovative
- Trustworthy
- Calm
- Professional
- Approachable

Avoid choosing traits simply because they sound impressive.

Choose characteristics you are committed to demonstrating consistently.

Step 4: Identify Your Unique Strengths
List your strongest professional advantages.
Consider:

- Skills
- Experience
- Education
- Personal interests
- Life experiences
- Technical expertise
- Communication style
- Creative abilities

Ask yourself:
"What do I consistently do well that creates value for others?"

Step 5: Define Your Audience
Describe the people you most want to serve.
Include:

- Age range (if relevant)
- Experience level
- Goals
- Common challenges
- Questions they frequently ask
- Problems they want solved

Understanding your audience allows you to communicate with greater clarity and purpose.

Step 6: Evaluate Your Current Brand

Review everything representing your professional identity.
Examples include:

- Website
- Books
- Social media
- Business cards
- Newsletters
- Emails
- Product descriptions
- Presentations

Ask:

- Does each element reflect my mission?
- Is my communication consistent?
- Does my work demonstrate professionalism?

Write improvements for each area.

Step 7: Strengthen Your Professional Communication
Review three recent emails, articles, or public communications.
Ask yourself:

- Were they clear?
- Were they respectful?
- Were they helpful?
- Did they reflect my values?

Rewrite anything that does not represent the professional identity you want to build.

Step 8: Create Your Signature Standards

Write a list of standards every project must meet before being released.

Examples:

- Carefully proofread.
- Fact-checked.
- Professionally formatted.
- Clearly organized.
- Helpful to the audience.
- Consistent with my mission.
- Delivered on time whenever reasonably possible.

These standards become your quality checklist.

Step 9: Ask for Constructive Feedback

Choose three trusted individuals.
Ask them:

- What three words describe my professional strengths?
- What do I do particularly well?
- Where could I improve?

Record every response without becoming defensive.
Look for recurring themes.

Step 10: Create a One-Year Growth Plan

Write five measurable goals for strengthening your brand.

Examples include:

- Publish three books.
- Complete two certifications.
- Improve my website.
- Launch a newsletter.
- Strengthen customer communication.
- Learn new technology.

Every goal should reinforce your long-term mission.

Step 11: Develop a Weekly Brand Review

Every week ask yourself:

- Did my actions reflect my values?
- Did I keep my promises?
- Did I improve my knowledge?
- Did I create meaningful value?
- Did I strengthen my reputation?

Write one improvement for the following week.

Step 12: Write Your Quantum Brand Commitment

Complete the following statement:

"My brand will always reflect my true character rather than artificial appearances. I will build trust through honesty, excellence, professionalism, continuous learning, thoughtful communication, and meaningful service. Every interaction will strengthen the reputation I am intentionally creating, one day at a time."

Read this commitment regularly to remind yourself that the strongest professional brands are built through consistent actions rather than temporary attention.

Why This Exercise Matters

A personal brand is one of the few assets that influences every opportunity you will ever encounter. It affects customer confidence, professional relationships, career opportunities, partnerships, referrals, and long-term reputation. By intentionally defining your mission, strengthening your communication, maintaining high standards, and consistently living according to your values, you create a brand that people naturally trust because it reflects genuine character rather than carefully manufactured appearances. **Over time, a reputation built on integrity, excellence, and consistent value becomes one of the most powerful and enduring forms of wealth you can ever create.**

Journal Prompts

1. What does **Quantum Branding** mean to me, and how has this chapter changed the way I think about building a professional reputation?
2. What three qualities do I want people to consistently associate with my name, and what daily actions will reinforce those qualities?
3. How well does my current work reflect my values, mission, and long-term vision, and where is there room for improvement?
4. Which professional habit would have the greatest positive impact on my reputation if I practiced it consistently every day?
5. How can I communicate more clearly, professionally, and authentically so that people immediately understand the value I provide?
6. Looking at everything I create—books, products, services, communication, and customer interactions—which area most needs improvement to better represent my brand?
7. What knowledge or skill should I develop over the next year that would significantly strengthen my credibility and long-term professional identity?
8. How can I build an ecosystem of valuable resources that continues helping people at different stages of their personal or professional journey?
9. If someone described my professional reputation ten years from now, what would I hope they would honestly say about my character, reliability, expertise, and contribution?
10. Beginning today, what one consistent action will I take every day to strengthen my reputation and ensure that my brand becomes synonymous with integrity, excellence, and meaningful value?

Closing Reflection

A powerful brand is not created through clever slogans, expensive advertising, or carefully manufactured appearances. It is created through thousands of consistent actions that demonstrate integrity, professionalism, competence, and genuine concern for the people you serve. Every conversation, every email, every book, every product, every promise you keep, and every problem you solve quietly shapes the story people associate with your name.

Throughout this chapter, you discovered that **Quantum Branding is ultimately the intentional alignment of your character, your communication, and the value you consistently create.** Rather than pursuing recognition for its own sake, you learned to focus on becoming someone whose work naturally earns confidence because it reflects honesty, excellence, and thoughtful service. Reputation is not built in a single moment—it is accumulated through countless ordinary decisions made with extraordinary consistency.

You also explored the importance of communicating value clearly, building trust before seeking opportunity, creating interconnected ecosystems instead of isolated products, and leading through contribution rather than status. These principles demonstrate that the strongest brands are not built upon appearances but upon repeated experiences that leave people feeling informed, respected, supported, and confident in your ability to deliver meaningful results.

Remember that **your name is one of your most valuable business assets.** Every project you complete either strengthens or weakens the reputation attached to it. Every customer interaction becomes part of your professional identity. Every commitment you honor quietly increases trust. Every lesson you learn improves the quality of everything you create in the future. Treat your reputation with the same care you would give your most valuable investment, because it influences opportunities that cannot always be measured financially.

As you continue through *Quantum Cashflow*, resist the temptation to build an image that is larger than reality. Instead, build a reality so consistently excellent that your reputation grows naturally through the quality of your work. Continue learning. Continue improving. Continue serving with integrity. Continue allowing your actions to speak more loudly than your claims.

When your character and your brand become indistinguishable, trust becomes your greatest competitive advantage. When trust combines with consistent excellence, meaningful value, and lifelong learning, your reputation becomes a lasting asset that continues opening doors, strengthening relationships, and creating opportunities for decades to come.

Chapter 8: Automating Financial Gravity—Creating an Unstoppable Flow of Cash

---

Designing Systems That Keep Creating Value

One of the greatest advantages of modern technology is that it allows thoughtfully designed systems to continue creating value long after the original work has been completed. The title of this chapter uses the phrase "**Automating Financial Gravity**" as a metaphor for building reliable systems that consistently support financial growth. It does **not** imply that money flows automatically without effort, responsibility, or ongoing stewardship. Rather, it describes the process of creating repeatable, dependable systems that reduce unnecessary manual work while allowing your knowledge, products, services, and assets to reach more people efficiently. **Automation strengthens value when it supports quality, consistency, and thoughtful service—not when it attempts to replace them.**

Every successful organization relies upon systems that operate consistently. Banks process transactions through automated infrastructure. Online retailers manage inventory and order fulfillment through sophisticated software. Educational platforms deliver lessons automatically according to scheduled programs. Publishers distribute digital books around the world through electronic marketplaces. Customer support systems organize communication efficiently. These examples demonstrate that automation is not about eliminating human contribution—it is about allowing people to spend less time repeating routine tasks and more time improving products, solving problems, and serving others creatively.

Before any process should be automated, it must first be understood. Many people attempt to automate inefficient systems, only to discover that they have simply increased the speed at which problems occur. Begin by carefully documenting each recurring task you perform. Which steps happen repeatedly? Which activities require little creative judgment? Which processes consume time without adding significant value?

Only after understanding the workflow should you consider simplifying or automating appropriate portions of it. **A well-designed manual system almost always becomes a better automated system than a poorly organized one.**

One of the greatest benefits of automation is consistency. Human attention naturally fluctuates because of fatigue, interruptions, competing priorities, and unexpected responsibilities. Thoughtfully designed systems reduce the likelihood that important recurring tasks will be forgotten. Appointment reminders, scheduled newsletters, recurring invoices, document templates, project management systems, customer follow-up sequences, inventory tracking, and digital file organization all help maintain dependable operations while reducing unnecessary mental effort. Consistency builds trust because people know what to expect every time they interact with your work.

Automation also creates additional time for activities requiring human creativity and judgment. Writing books, designing educational resources, mentoring others, conducting research, solving complex problems, strengthening customer relationships, and developing innovative ideas all require thoughtful attention that technology cannot fully replace. By allowing software to manage routine administrative responsibilities, you preserve more of your energy for the work that creates the greatest long-term value. **Technology performs best when supporting human creativity rather than attempting to replace it.**

Financial gravity becomes stronger as systems begin supporting one another. A website introduces visitors to valuable resources. Automated email sequences provide educational content. Digital products are delivered immediately after purchase. Customer questions are organized efficiently. Financial records update automatically. Inventory systems track availability. Each component contributes to a larger ecosystem in which information flows smoothly from one process to the next. Rather than functioning independently, these systems cooperate to create a more reliable experience for both the creator and the customer.

It is equally important to remember that automation requires ongoing supervision. Systems should be reviewed regularly to ensure they remain accurate, secure, relevant, and aligned with current goals. Customer needs change. Technologies evolve. Security standards improve. Educational materials require updates. Automated processes should never be ignored simply because they appear to function independently. Responsible stewardship includes monitoring performance, correcting errors promptly, and continually improving the quality of every system supporting your work. **Automation succeeds when guided by thoughtful oversight rather than passive neglect.**

As you begin this chapter, remember that the objective is not to create money without effort. The true objective is to build systems that consistently create, deliver, and protect value while allowing you to focus on your highest contributions. Whether you are an author, educator, entrepreneur, consultant, investor, or professional in any field, thoughtful automation allows your work to become more organized, more dependable, and more scalable. **When reliable systems consistently support meaningful value creation, financial momentum becomes easier to sustain because your daily effort is strengthened by processes designed to continue working alongside you rather than depending entirely upon you.**

Building Financial Systems That Work Every Day

One of the most valuable shifts a person can make is moving from managing finances through memory to managing them through dependable systems. Memory is useful, but it is easily interrupted by busy schedules, unexpected responsibilities, and changing priorities. Systems provide consistency because they continue operating according to clearly defined processes rather than momentary motivation. **Financial stability grows stronger when important responsibilities depend on reliable systems instead of perfect memory.**

A strong financial system begins with organization. Every source of income, recurring expense, investment account, savings goal, insurance policy, business asset, and financial obligation should be documented clearly. Organized information allows better decisions because you are working from accurate knowledge rather than assumptions. When financial records are scattered across notebooks, email folders, paper files, and disconnected applications, valuable time is often spent searching for information instead of using it productively. A well-organized financial system transforms information into a practical decision-making tool.

Another important component is creating repeatable routines. Monthly financial reviews, scheduled invoice processing, recurring savings contributions, regular investment evaluations, quarterly business planning, and annual goal assessments help ensure that important responsibilities receive consistent attention. Rather than waiting until problems arise, these routines encourage proactive management. Small adjustments made regularly often prevent much larger difficulties later. **Consistent review strengthens financial confidence because you remain informed rather than surprised.**

Automation can strengthen these routines when applied thoughtfully. Automatic bill payments reduce the risk of unnecessary late fees. Scheduled transfers help build emergency savings gradually. Recurring retirement or investment contributions encourage long-term consistency. Digital accounting software organizes financial records efficiently. Calendar reminders ensure important reviews are not overlooked.

These systems support responsible financial habits by reducing repetitive administrative work while keeping essential responsibilities visible. Technology becomes most valuable when it reinforces wise decisions that have already been made intentionally.

Strong financial systems also include regular measurement. Businesses monitor revenue, expenses, customer satisfaction, and operational efficiency because meaningful improvement requires accurate information. Individuals benefit from similar practices. Tracking progress toward savings goals, reviewing monthly spending patterns, evaluating investment performance responsibly, and measuring business growth all provide valuable insights. Measurement should never become an obsession; its purpose is to support informed decision-making and continuous improvement rather than constant worry.

Flexibility remains essential within every financial system. Circumstances change throughout life. New opportunities appear. Unexpected expenses occur. Economic conditions evolve. Effective systems should be reviewed and adjusted whenever meaningful changes occur. A budget created several years ago may no longer reflect current priorities. Business workflows may require updates as technology improves. Investment strategies should be evaluated according to changing objectives and appropriate professional guidance when necessary. **A strong system remains structured while still allowing thoughtful adaptation to changing circumstances.**

Documentation strengthens every financial process. Written procedures, organized records, standardized checklists, and clearly defined workflows make recurring tasks easier to repeat accurately. Documentation also simplifies collaboration with accountants, financial advisors, business partners, employees, or family members when appropriate. Instead of relying upon memory, documented systems preserve knowledge while reducing unnecessary confusion. Every improvement recorded today saves time and increases consistency tomorrow.

As your systems become more dependable, financial decisions often become less stressful. Instead of reacting constantly to immediate concerns, you gain greater confidence because essential responsibilities are already supported by thoughtful processes. Savings continue growing through consistent contributions. Records remain organized. Reviews occur regularly. Opportunities become easier to evaluate because accurate information is readily available. **Financial gravity develops not through dramatic moments but through hundreds of reliable systems quietly working together every day. Each organized process strengthens the next, creating a stable foundation capable of supporting long-term growth, resilience, and lasting prosperity.**

Connecting Your Income Streams Into One Financial Ecosystem

One of the most effective ways to strengthen long-term financial momentum is to stop thinking of each source of income as an isolated event. Instead, begin viewing every source of value as part of a larger financial ecosystem in which each component supports the others. A book can introduce readers to additional educational resources. A consulting engagement may inspire future workshops. A digital course can complement a published guide. An investment portfolio may provide stability while a business continues expanding. **When your financial activities are intentionally connected, they become stronger together than they would be independently.**

A financial ecosystem begins with a central mission rather than a collection of unrelated opportunities. Ask yourself, **"What is the primary value I create?"** Once that answer becomes clear, every additional income stream should strengthen that mission instead of distracting from it. An educator might build books, courses, speaking engagements, and consulting services around one area of expertise. A designer may combine creative services, templates, educational resources, and licensing opportunities. The goal is not simply to create more products but to create a family of resources that naturally reinforce one another.

Each part of the ecosystem should perform a specific role. Some resources introduce people to your work. Others provide deeper education. Some solve immediate problems, while others offer ongoing support or advanced knowledge. Certain products generate recurring income, while others establish credibility or strengthen long-term relationships. Understanding the purpose of every component helps eliminate unnecessary duplication while ensuring that each resource contributes meaningfully to the overall system. **Every part should strengthen the whole rather than compete with it.**

Thoughtful organization makes this ecosystem easier for both you and your audience to navigate. Clear pathways allow people to understand what should come next after completing one resource. Someone reading an introductory book may naturally progress to a workbook, online course, advanced guide, or professional consultation. Customers appreciate logical progression because it reduces confusion and helps them continue learning at a comfortable pace. A well-organized ecosystem demonstrates intentional planning rather than random expansion.

Automation strengthens these connections by ensuring information flows consistently between systems. A customer purchasing a book may automatically receive helpful educational resources. Newsletter subscribers may receive carefully scheduled learning materials. Course participants can receive reminders, updates, and additional guidance without requiring every message to be written manually. Customer support systems organize inquiries efficiently while maintaining professional communication. **Automation should strengthen relationships by making valuable information easier to deliver, not by replacing genuine human care.**

An interconnected ecosystem also creates resilience during changing market conditions. If one source of income experiences temporary challenges, other components continue supporting overall stability. Books continue introducing readers. Educational resources continue serving students. Consulting relationships remain active. Investments continue following their long-term objectives. Each part contributes differently while supporting the same overall mission. Diversification becomes more effective because every component shares a common purpose instead of existing as unrelated projects.

Reviewing the ecosystem regularly is just as important as building it. Markets evolve, customer needs change, technologies improve, and your own expertise expands over time. Evaluate how well each component serves its intended purpose. Which resources generate the greatest value? Which systems require improvement? Which products complement one another effectively? Continuous refinement keeps the ecosystem healthy while preventing unnecessary complexity. Simplicity often creates greater long-term strength than endless expansion.

As you continue developing **Automating Financial Gravity**, remember that lasting financial momentum rarely comes from isolated successes. It grows through carefully designed systems that cooperate, reinforce one another, and continue creating value consistently over time. Every asset, every workflow, every customer relationship, every educational resource, and every thoughtful improvement becomes another part of a larger structure designed for long-term sustainability. **When your financial activities function as one connected ecosystem instead of separate projects, momentum begins building naturally because every part contributes to the strength, resilience, and long-term growth of the entire system.**

Compounding Small Improvements Into Extraordinary Results

Many people imagine financial success as the result of one breakthrough idea, one life-changing investment, or one extraordinary opportunity. While significant moments certainly occur, lasting prosperity is more often built through the quiet accumulation of hundreds of small improvements repeated consistently over time. Every system refined, every skill strengthened, every expense managed wisely, every customer experience improved, every process simplified, and every lesson applied contributes to a gradual increase in effectiveness. **Financial gravity becomes stronger because progress compounds, not because perfection suddenly appears.**

The principle of compounding extends far beyond investing. Knowledge compounds each time you study and apply what you learn. Writing ability improves with every completed page. Professional relationships deepen through years of consistent trust. Business systems become more efficient as they are refined. Customer loyalty grows through repeated positive experiences. Personal discipline strengthens every time you honor your commitments. Individually, these improvements may appear modest. Collectively, they create extraordinary long-term momentum because each improvement supports the next.

One useful habit is asking a simple question at the end of every workday: **"What one thing can I improve before tomorrow?"** The answer does not need to involve dramatic change. Perhaps a checklist could become clearer. A document could be organized more effectively. A frequently asked question could become part of a knowledge base. A repetitive task might be simplified through automation. A customer email could be rewritten for greater clarity. These seemingly minor refinements gradually transform the overall quality of your work. **Excellence is often the accumulated result of countless small decisions rather than occasional extraordinary effort.**

Compounding also depends upon consistency. Improving a process once is valuable, but reviewing it regularly ensures it continues serving its purpose as circumstances evolve. Markets change. Technology advances. Customer expectations develop. Financial goals mature. Systems that remain static eventually become outdated. Individuals and organizations committed to continuous improvement recognize that refinement is an ongoing practice rather than a one-time event. Every review creates another opportunity to strengthen quality, efficiency, and long-term resilience.

Documentation accelerates the compounding process because it preserves lessons learned. Recording successful workflows, effective strategies, common mistakes, and practical solutions prevents valuable knowledge from being forgotten. Instead of repeatedly solving the same problems, documented experience becomes a growing library of wisdom that supports future decisions. Teams benefit from this shared knowledge, and individuals save time because previous insights remain accessible whenever needed. **Learning compounds most effectively when it is captured, organized, and reviewed regularly.**

Feedback is another powerful source of continuous improvement. Customers, readers, colleagues, mentors, and trusted advisors often recognize opportunities that may be difficult to see from within your own work. Constructive feedback should be welcomed rather than feared because it provides valuable information for refinement. Listening carefully, evaluating suggestions thoughtfully, and implementing meaningful improvements demonstrate humility while strengthening the overall quality of your systems. Every thoughtful adjustment increases the value you are able to provide.

Patience remains essential throughout this process. The benefits of continuous improvement rarely become obvious after a single day or even a single month. However, after several years of consistent refinement, the difference becomes remarkable. A business with improved systems operates more efficiently. A professional who studies regularly develops greater expertise. A writer who revises carefully produces stronger books. An investor who follows disciplined principles benefits from long-term growth. **Small improvements become extraordinary**

results because time allows them to accumulate beyond what seems possible in the beginning.

As you continue building **Automating Financial Gravity**, remember that your greatest competitive advantage may not be one revolutionary innovation but your willingness to improve steadily when others become comfortable with "good enough." Continue refining your systems. Continue strengthening your knowledge. Continue documenting your lessons. Continue welcoming thoughtful feedback. Every improvement, however modest, becomes another force contributing to long-term momentum. **When small refinements are applied consistently over months and years, they create a powerful form of financial gravity that supports lasting success through continuous excellence rather than temporary bursts of effort.**

Stewarding Financial Momentum for a Lifetime

Creating financial momentum is a significant achievement, but preserving and strengthening that momentum over decades requires an entirely different mindset. Many people focus intensely on acquiring income yet devote far less attention to maintaining the systems that produced it. The purpose of **Automating Financial Gravity** is not simply to help you build financial movement—it is to help you create momentum that remains stable, adaptable, and valuable throughout changing seasons of life. **Lasting prosperity depends as much upon stewardship as it does upon creation.**

Stewardship begins with recognizing that every financial resource carries responsibility. Income should be managed thoughtfully. Assets deserve regular maintenance. Business systems require review. Professional skills need continual development. Customer relationships benefit from ongoing attention. Investments should be evaluated responsibly according to long-term objectives and, when appropriate, with qualified professional guidance. Every valuable resource becomes stronger when it receives consistent care rather than occasional attention. **What is managed intentionally tends to remain healthier than what is simply left alone.**

Long-term momentum also requires resisting unnecessary complexity. As businesses grow, new opportunities naturally appear. Additional products, technologies, partnerships, and systems can all contribute positively, but they can also create confusion if added without careful consideration. Periodically ask yourself whether every process still serves a meaningful purpose. Are there unnecessary steps that could be simplified? Have outdated systems remained in place simply because they have always existed? Simplicity often improves reliability because fewer moving parts generally require less maintenance while remaining easier to understand and improve.

Another important aspect of stewardship is preparing for change before change becomes necessary. Technologies evolve. Customer expectations shift. Economic conditions fluctuate. Personal priorities may also develop over time. Rather than waiting until existing systems become ineffective, thoughtful leaders regularly evaluate emerging trends, continue learning, and prepare gradual improvements. This proactive approach reduces disruption because adjustments occur through careful planning instead of emergency reactions. **Preparation transforms uncertainty into opportunity by allowing change to be approached deliberately rather than fearfully.**

Financial momentum also benefits from healthy personal habits. Physical well-being, emotional resilience, intellectual curiosity, meaningful relationships, and appropriate periods of rest all influence your ability to continue creating value over the long term. Sustainable success is rarely achieved by sacrificing every other area of life indefinitely. Instead, balance supports longevity because creativity, sound judgment, and thoughtful leadership depend upon a healthy foundation. The strongest financial systems are ultimately supported by individuals who care responsibly for their own capacity to lead, learn, and contribute.

Generosity plays an important role in sustaining momentum as well. Sharing knowledge, mentoring others, supporting worthwhile causes, strengthening professional communities, and helping people solve meaningful problems often expands opportunities in ways that cannot always be predicted or measured immediately. Generosity should never be viewed merely as a strategy for financial gain. Rather, it reflects an understanding that value grows stronger when it contributes positively to the lives of others. **Communities thrive when individuals consistently invest in the success and well-being of those around them.**

Reflection should become a regular part of every financial system. Set aside time to review not only financial performance but also the broader impact of your work. Ask whether your systems remain aligned with your values. Consider whether your projects continue solving meaningful problems. Evaluate whether your reputation reflects the character you intend to demonstrate. Reflection transforms experience into wisdom because it encourages thoughtful learning instead of automatic repetition. Every review creates another opportunity to strengthen both your results and your purpose.

As you complete this chapter, remember that financial gravity is not created by one successful project, one fortunate investment, or one exceptional year. It is created through a lifetime of thoughtful stewardship, continuous improvement, disciplined systems, responsible adaptation, and meaningful contribution. Continue refining your processes. Continue strengthening your knowledge. Continue serving others with integrity. Continue protecting the trust that supports every opportunity you receive. **When your financial systems are guided by wisdom, consistency, adaptability, and purpose, they become more than mechanisms for generating income—they become enduring foundations capable of supporting lasting prosperity, meaningful service, and a legacy of responsible leadership for many years to come.**

Exercise 1: Build Your Financial Automation Blueprint

The purpose of this exercise is to help you design a practical financial system that consistently creates value while reducing unnecessary manual effort. The goal is not to automate every part of your life or business. Instead, it is to identify the repetitive processes that can be organized, simplified, and supported through reliable systems, allowing you to devote more attention to creativity, strategic thinking, learning, and serving others. **Automation should always strengthen your ability to create meaningful value—not replace the thoughtful work that only you can do.**

Step 1: Document Every Repeating Financial Activity

Spend thirty minutes listing every recurring financial task you perform.

Examples include:

- Paying bills
- Sending invoices
- Tracking expenses
- Reviewing investments
- Updating accounting records
- Publishing content
- Responding to customer emails
- Organizing receipts
- Monitoring subscriptions
- Reviewing monthly reports

Do not evaluate the list yet.

Simply capture every repeating activity.

Step 2: Categorize Your Activities

Divide every task into three categories:

Daily

Weekly

Monthly

This simple organization immediately reveals where your time is currently being invested.

–

Step 3: Identify Repetitive Tasks
Highlight every activity that follows nearly identical steps each time. Examples:

- Invoice creation
- Appointment reminders
- File organization
- Monthly financial reviews
- Customer onboarding
- Newsletter scheduling

These activities often provide excellent opportunities for automation or standardization.

Step 4: Write the Current Workflow

Choose one repetitive task.

Document every step exactly as you currently perform it.

Avoid skipping details.

You cannot improve a process you have not clearly defined.

Step 5: Remove Unnecessary Steps

Review your workflow carefully.
Ask yourself:

- Which steps create little value?
- Which actions are duplicated?
- Which decisions happen repeatedly without good reason?
- Which information could be entered only once?

Simplification should always occur before automation.

Step 6: Choose Helpful Technology
Identify tools that could support the improved process.
Examples include:

- Calendar automation
- Accounting software
- Project management systems
- Cloud storage
- Customer relationship management software
- Email scheduling
- Digital payment systems
- Workflow automation platforms

Select technology because it solves a real problem—not simply because it is available.

Step 7: Create One Standard Operating Procedure

Write a simple document describing exactly how this task should be completed.

Include:

- Purpose
- Required information
- Sequence of steps
- Expected outcome

Clear documentation improves consistency while making future improvements easier.

Step 8: Build a Review Schedule
Decide how often the process should be evaluated.
Examples:

- Monthly
- Quarterly
- Twice each year

Technology changes.
Businesses evolve.
Systems should improve regularly.

Step 9: Measure the Results

After implementing your improved system, record:

- Time saved
- Errors reduced
- Customer experience improvements
- Organizational improvements
- Financial benefits

Measurement allows you to verify that the system is producing meaningful results.

Step 10: Repeat With Another Process

After successfully improving one workflow, choose another.

Avoid trying to automate everything simultaneously.

Small improvements accumulate into remarkable long-term efficiency.

Step 11: Create Your Financial Dashboard

Design a simple summary page containing your most important financial indicators.

Examples include:

- Monthly income
- Monthly expenses
- Savings progress
- Investment contributions
- Business revenue
- Outstanding invoices
- Cash reserves

Review this dashboard regularly instead of searching through multiple reports.

Step 12: Write Your Automation Commitment

Complete the following statement:

"I will build thoughtful systems that strengthen my ability to create meaningful value. I will simplify before automating, review before expanding, improve before replacing, and use technology responsibly to support excellence, consistency, and long-term financial stewardship."

Read this commitment whenever introducing a new workflow, software system, or financial process.

Why This Exercise Matters

Automation is not about eliminating effort—it is about directing your effort toward the activities that matter most. Every repetitive task you simplify, every system you improve, every workflow you document, and every financial process you organize creates additional capacity for creativity, learning, innovation, and meaningful service. Over time, these improvements compound into a business and financial life that is more organized, resilient, efficient, and adaptable. **When thoughtfully designed systems quietly support your daily work, financial momentum becomes easier to maintain because your success is strengthened by reliable processes working alongside your consistent effort.**

Journal Prompts

1. What does **Automating Financial Gravity** mean to me, and how has this chapter changed the way I think about creating long-term financial momentum?
2. Which repetitive financial or business task consumes the most time in my life, and how could I simplify or systematize it?
3. Looking at my current financial habits, where am I relying too heavily on memory instead of dependable systems?
4. Which areas of my personal or professional life would benefit most from better organization, documentation, or automation?
5. What systems am I already using successfully, and what lessons can I apply from those systems to improve other areas of my financial life?
6. How can I better connect my books, products, services, investments, or professional activities into one unified financial ecosystem?
7. What one-percent improvement can I make this week that will strengthen my financial systems over the long term?
8. How can I use technology more intentionally to increase efficiency while still maintaining personal relationships, excellent customer service, and high-quality work?
9. If I reviewed my financial systems five years from now, what would I hope has become completely organized, dependable, and self-sustaining?
10. Beginning today, what one system will I build, improve, or automate that will continue creating value and supporting my financial goals for years to come?

Closing Reflection

Financial success is rarely sustained through effort alone. It is sustained through systems that consistently support wise decisions, organized workflows, dependable communication, thoughtful stewardship, and continuous improvement. While discipline remains essential, discipline becomes far more effective when it is reinforced by reliable processes that reduce unnecessary complexity and allow you to focus your energy where it creates the greatest value.

Throughout this chapter, you discovered that **Automating Financial Gravity is not about removing yourself from the work—it is about removing unnecessary friction from the work.** Every organized workflow, every documented procedure, every thoughtful automation, every financial review, and every interconnected system strengthens your ability to serve others while building a more resilient financial foundation. Technology becomes most valuable when it supports your judgment, creativity, and integrity rather than attempting to replace them.

You also learned that lasting financial momentum grows through organization, consistency, continuous refinement, and responsible oversight. Automation without planning creates confusion. Systems without review become outdated. Growth without structure becomes difficult to sustain. But when every process is intentionally designed, regularly evaluated, and continually improved, small daily efficiencies begin compounding into extraordinary long-term results.

Remember that **financial gravity is created one system at a time.** Every recurring task you simplify saves future time. Every workflow you improve increases consistency. Every asset you connect into a larger ecosystem strengthens the whole. Every lesson you document prevents future mistakes. Every thoughtful review creates another opportunity to refine the foundation beneath your financial life. These improvements may seem small in isolation, but together they become a powerful force that quietly supports progress every single day.

As you continue your journey through *Quantum Cashflow*, challenge yourself to think like a system designer rather than simply a task completer. Ask yourself regularly:

- **What process can I simplify?**
- **What workflow can I improve?**
- **What system can I document?**
- **What recurring responsibility can I organize more effectively?**
- **How can today's improvement continue creating value tomorrow?**

The answers to these questions will gradually transform scattered effort into purposeful momentum.

When your financial life is supported by thoughtful systems, guided by continuous improvement, strengthened through responsible automation, and anchored in meaningful value creation, you develop a form of financial gravity that becomes increasingly difficult to stop. Consistent systems create consistent progress, consistent progress builds lasting momentum, and lasting momentum becomes the quiet force behind enduring prosperity.

Chapter 9: Energy-to-Wealth Conversion—The Hidden Law of Manifesting Money

---

Directing Your Energy Toward Value Creation

Every financial result begins long before money changes hands. It begins with attention, intention, learning, disciplined effort, thoughtful decisions, and consistent action. Throughout history, individuals have transformed ideas into inventions, knowledge into education, creativity into art, and expertise into businesses because they deliberately invested their personal energy in creating value for others. In this chapter, the phrase **"Energy-to-Wealth Conversion"** is used as a metaphor for this process. It describes the intentional transformation of your time, focus, skills, and persistence into products, services, relationships, and opportunities that can generate financial value. **The hidden law is not a mystical force—it is the practical reality that focused effort directed toward meaningful value creation often produces opportunities that scattered effort does not.**

Every person possesses the same twenty-four hours each day, yet those hours produce dramatically different outcomes depending upon how they are invested. Some energy is spent reacting to interruptions, distractions, and unnecessary obligations. Other energy is invested in learning, building systems, strengthening relationships, solving problems, and creating assets that continue serving others. The difference is not simply how hard someone works but where that work is directed. **Focused energy generally produces greater long-term results than unfocused activity because intention gives effort a clear destination.**

Attention is one of your most valuable forms of personal capital. Wherever your attention consistently goes, your skills, habits, and opportunities gradually follow. If your attention is continually divided among distractions, meaningful progress becomes difficult because creative work requires sustained concentration. Conversely, when you regularly devote focused time to improving your craft, developing valuable assets, strengthening professional relationships, and solving worthwhile problems, those efforts accumulate into knowledge and experience that continue increasing your ability to create value. **Attention is the bridge between intention and achievement because it determines what receives your consistent effort.**

Mental energy also influences the quality of your decisions. Fatigue, constant multitasking, and chronic distraction often reduce creativity and thoughtful judgment. Protecting periods of uninterrupted focus allows you to think more deeply, solve problems more effectively, and produce higher-quality work. This is one reason the ten-minute principle introduced earlier in this book remains so powerful. Even a brief period of concentrated attention, repeated consistently over months and years, can produce remarkable growth because it strengthens habits that compound over time.

Energy is also expressed through emotion. Enthusiasm encourages learning. Curiosity invites exploration. Patience supports long-term projects. Resilience allows you to continue after setbacks. These qualities do not magically attract money, but they strongly influence the behaviors that often lead to greater opportunities. Someone who approaches challenges with curiosity is more likely to continue learning. Someone who remains resilient after disappointment is more likely to complete important projects. **Constructive emotional habits support productive actions, and productive actions create opportunities for meaningful financial growth.**

Every meaningful asset begins as an investment of energy before it becomes an investment of money. Books require research, writing, editing, and revision. Businesses require planning, experimentation, customer service, and continuous improvement. Professional expertise develops through study and practical experience. Relationships strengthen through thoughtful communication and consistent trust. None of these assets appear instantly, yet each represents accumulated effort transformed into lasting value. Over time, these assets may continue creating opportunities long after the original work has been completed.

An important part of Energy-to-Wealth Conversion is eliminating activities that consume energy without creating corresponding value. This does not mean avoiding recreation, family, or rest—all of which contribute to a balanced and sustainable life. Rather, it means recognizing recurring habits that repeatedly drain attention while moving you no closer to your long-term objectives. Identifying unnecessary friction creates additional capacity for learning, creating, improving, and serving. **Protecting your energy is just as important as investing it because depleted attention rarely produces exceptional work.**

As you begin this chapter, remember that lasting prosperity is not created by wishing, hoping, or waiting for circumstances to change. It grows when you intentionally direct your knowledge, creativity, discipline, and focused effort toward solving meaningful problems and creating lasting value. Every page you write, every skill you strengthen, every relationship you nurture, every system you improve, and every thoughtful decision you make becomes another example of Energy-to-Wealth Conversion. **When your daily energy is invested consistently in creating value, opportunities often grow because your capacity to contribute continues expanding year after year.**

The Multiplier Effect of Focused Attention

One of the greatest misconceptions about productivity is that doing more things automatically creates better results. In reality, sustained progress is more often the result of concentrated attention applied to a few meaningful priorities rather than scattered attention divided among countless activities. Every time your focus shifts unnecessarily, your mind spends valuable energy regaining concentration. Over weeks, months, and years, these interruptions quietly reduce the amount of meaningful work completed. **Focused attention multiplies the effectiveness of your effort because it allows your knowledge, creativity, and judgment to work together without constant interruption.**

Your attention functions much like a valuable investment portfolio. Every hour represents capital that can be invested intentionally or spent carelessly. Hours devoted to learning valuable skills, strengthening relationships, creating assets, refining systems, and solving important problems often continue producing benefits far into the future. Hours repeatedly consumed by unnecessary distractions rarely provide similar long-term returns. This observation is not intended to eliminate leisure or recreation, both of which contribute to health and creativity. Instead, it encourages thoughtful awareness of how your limited attention is allocated. **Your future is influenced by the recurring destinations of your attention more than by isolated moments of intense effort.**

High-value work usually requires uninterrupted thinking. Writing a book, designing software, conducting research, developing educational resources, planning a business strategy, or solving a complex challenge all demand periods of sustained concentration. These activities often create disproportionately valuable results because they combine knowledge, creativity, and experience into something new that continues serving others. Protecting uninterrupted time for this kind of work is one of the most effective ways to increase your long-term capacity for value creation.

The quality of your environment also influences your attention. A workspace filled with constant notifications, unnecessary clutter, competing conversations, or frequent interruptions makes deep concentration more difficult. By organizing your workspace, silencing unnecessary alerts, preparing materials in advance, and scheduling focused work periods, you reduce friction that competes for your mental energy. Small environmental improvements often produce significant gains because they remove obstacles before they interrupt your thinking. **A well-designed environment quietly supports better decisions and higher-quality work every day.**

Intentional planning further strengthens focused attention. Beginning each day with a small number of clearly defined priorities reduces decision fatigue because you already know where your energy should be directed. Rather than reacting continuously to whatever demands immediate attention, you establish meaningful objectives before distractions arise. This approach creates greater clarity while helping ensure that your most valuable work receives your highest level of concentration rather than whatever energy remains afterward.

Another important aspect of focused attention is learning to complete meaningful work before seeking constant feedback or approval. Creative projects often require periods of uninterrupted development before they are ready for evaluation. Continually checking reactions, comparing progress with others, or switching between multiple unfinished tasks can reduce both confidence and productivity. Instead, commit to finishing meaningful portions of your work before pausing to review, revise, or seek constructive input. **Completion creates momentum because finished work can be improved, while unfinished work often remains only potential.**

Focused attention also compounds through habit. The more consistently you practice concentrated work, the easier it becomes to enter periods of deep thinking. Your mind gradually adapts to sustained concentration just as your body adapts to regular physical exercise. What initially feels difficult often becomes increasingly natural through repetition. Over time, this ability to focus becomes a significant professional advantage because it allows you to produce thoughtful, high-quality work while others remain trapped in constant distraction.

As you continue exploring **Energy-to-Wealth Conversion**, remember that your attention is one of the few resources that cannot be expanded beyond the hours available each day. Every moment invested intentionally strengthens your knowledge, your skills, your relationships, your systems, and your ability to create value. Guard your attention carefully. Direct it purposefully. Review it regularly. **When focused attention becomes a daily habit, your effort gains a multiplying effect, allowing the same amount of time to produce greater wisdom, stronger assets, and more meaningful opportunities throughout your life.**

Transforming Knowledge Into Lasting Financial Value

Knowledge is one of the few resources that increases rather than decreases when it is used wisely. Every book you study, every skill you practice, every conversation with an experienced mentor, every lesson learned through success or failure, and every thoughtful observation becomes part of a growing foundation that influences your future decisions. By itself, knowledge has potential. When it is organized, applied, and shared to solve meaningful problems, it becomes a source of lasting value. **Energy-to-Wealth Conversion occurs when learning is transformed into practical action that improves the lives of others.**

Many people spend years accumulating information without ever applying it. They attend seminars, purchase courses, read books, collect certifications, and bookmark articles, yet little changes because knowledge remains inactive. Learning reaches its greatest value when it influences behavior. A financial principle becomes valuable when it improves budgeting. A communication technique becomes valuable when it strengthens relationships. A marketing lesson becomes valuable when it helps people discover useful products. **Information becomes an asset only after it is translated into consistent action.**

Application should always precede accumulation. Before searching for another resource, ask yourself whether you have fully implemented what you already know. One practical lesson consistently applied often produces greater long-term results than dozens of theories left unused. This approach encourages mastery rather than endless consumption. Instead of measuring progress by how much information you gather, measure it by how effectively you apply that information to create meaningful improvements.

Knowledge becomes even more valuable when it is organized into systems. Personal notes, documented workflows, research summaries, instructional guides, checklists, templates, and educational resources preserve what you have learned while making it easier to apply consistently. Organized knowledge also becomes easier to improve over time because new insights can be incorporated into an existing framework rather than scattered across disconnected sources. **A well-organized body of knowledge continues creating value long after the original lesson has been learned.**

Teaching is another powerful form of Energy-to-Wealth Conversion. Explaining ideas to others often reveals gaps in your own understanding while strengthening concepts already mastered. Whether you write books, mentor colleagues, create educational materials, lead workshops, or simply help someone solve a practical problem, teaching transforms personal knowledge into shared value. As others benefit from your experience, your own understanding frequently becomes deeper and more refined. Learning and teaching strengthen one another through continuous interaction.

Continuous learning also protects long-term relevance. Industries evolve, technologies improve, research advances, and customer needs change. Professionals who remain curious adapt more effectively because they continue expanding their understanding instead of relying solely upon past success. Lifelong learning is not a sign that previous knowledge was insufficient; it is recognition that excellence requires continual refinement. **The willingness to keep learning is often one of the strongest indicators of future growth because it allows your value to evolve alongside the world around you.**

Another important principle is recognizing that every experience contains knowledge worth preserving. Successful projects reveal effective strategies. Difficult projects reveal opportunities for improvement. Customer questions highlight areas requiring greater clarity. Unexpected challenges often produce innovative solutions. Instead of viewing experiences as isolated events, begin treating them as valuable sources of future wisdom. Reflection transforms experience into practical knowledge that continues supporting better decisions year after year.

As you continue developing the principles of **Energy-to-Wealth Conversion**, remember that your greatest financial assets may not begin as money at all. They often begin as ideas, observations, lessons, skills, relationships, and carefully developed expertise. Invest in learning with intention. Apply what you discover consistently. Organize your knowledge thoughtfully. Share it generously when appropriate. Continue refining it throughout your lifetime. **When knowledge is continually transformed into practical value, your personal energy creates benefits that extend far beyond today's work, strengthening your ability to contribute meaningfully while expanding opportunities for lasting financial growth.**

Purpose as a Multiplier of Productive Energy

One of the most overlooked sources of sustainable productivity is purpose. While motivation often rises and falls depending upon circumstances, purpose provides a more stable reason to continue learning, creating, and improving even when progress appears slow. Purpose answers the question, **"Why does this work matter?"** When that answer becomes clear, ordinary tasks gain greater significance because they contribute to something larger than immediate results. **Purpose does not replace discipline, but it gives discipline a meaningful direction.**

Many people begin ambitious projects with enthusiasm only to abandon them when difficulties arise. The challenge is rarely a lack of ability; more often, it is a lack of connection between daily work and long-term meaning. Writing one page may seem insignificant when viewed alone. However, that same page becomes meaningful when understood as part of a book that may educate readers for years. Improving one business process may appear ordinary until viewed as one step toward creating a more reliable organization. Purpose allows small daily actions to become part of a much larger vision.

Purpose also improves decision-making by providing a consistent standard for evaluating opportunities. Throughout every career, countless possibilities compete for your attention. Some promise immediate rewards but contribute little to your long-term objectives. Others require patience while supporting your deeper mission. When your purpose is clearly defined, decisions become easier because you can ask a simple question: **"Does this opportunity move me closer to the work I most want to accomplish?"** This approach reduces unnecessary distractions while helping preserve your limited time and energy.

Another advantage of purpose is resilience. Every meaningful project encounters setbacks, revisions, delays, and unexpected obstacles. Individuals driven only by immediate results may become discouraged during these periods. Those guided by a clear sense of purpose often continue because they recognize that temporary difficulties do not diminish the importance of the larger mission. Resilience grows stronger when challenges are understood as part of a worthwhile journey rather than evidence that the journey should end.

Purpose also influences the quality of your work. When you genuinely care about improving the lives of the people you serve, attention to detail naturally increases. You become more willing to revise, research carefully, improve communication, strengthen customer support, and refine systems because excellence supports the mission you value. Customers, readers, clients, and colleagues often recognize this commitment even if they cannot easily explain why. **Work guided by genuine purpose frequently communicates a level of care that cannot be manufactured through appearance alone.**

Your purpose should remain flexible enough to grow alongside your experience. Early in your career, your mission may focus on mastering a particular skill. Later, it may expand to include mentoring others, strengthening communities, advancing research, or creating lasting educational resources. While specific goals may evolve, the underlying commitment to creating meaningful value remains consistent. Continuous reflection helps ensure that your work continues aligning with what matters most rather than simply following familiar routines.

It is equally important to balance purpose with sustainability. A meaningful mission should inspire consistent effort without encouraging exhaustion or neglect of personal well-being. Rest, learning, family, friendships, recreation, and physical health all contribute to your long-term ability to continue serving others effectively. Sustainable purpose recognizes that your greatest contributions are strengthened—not weakened—when supported by a balanced and healthy life. **Protecting your ability to contribute tomorrow is part of fulfilling your purpose today.**

As you continue exploring **Energy-to-Wealth Conversion**, remember that purpose acts as a multiplier rather than a substitute for effort. It gives direction to your attention, strengthens resilience during challenges, improves decision-making, and encourages excellence because every task contributes to something meaningful. Clarify why your work matters. Revisit that purpose regularly. Allow it to guide your priorities, your learning, your systems, and your daily actions. **When your energy is consistently directed by a clear and meaningful purpose, your work gains lasting significance, your contribution deepens, and your ability to create enduring value continues expanding throughout every stage of your life.**

Sustaining High-Value Energy Through Wise Stewardship

Creating meaningful financial value requires more than knowledge, discipline, and purpose—it also requires protecting the physical, mental, and emotional capacity that allows you to continue creating that value over the long term. Many talented individuals begin ambitious projects with extraordinary enthusiasm only to discover that constant exhaustion gradually reduces the quality of their thinking, creativity, decision-making, and leadership. **Energy-to-Wealth Conversion depends not only on how much effort you invest but also on how wisely you manage the energy that makes that effort possible.**

Every day presents countless demands upon your attention. Meetings, emails, family responsibilities, financial decisions, creative projects, unexpected interruptions, and personal obligations all compete for limited mental resources. Because your attention is finite, stewardship becomes essential. Learning to distinguish between activities that genuinely create long-term value and those that merely consume time allows you to direct your highest levels of energy toward your most important work. This is not about becoming busy every moment of the day—it is about becoming intentional with the moments that matter most.

Physical well-being quietly supports every financial goal. Regular movement, sufficient sleep, balanced nutrition, appropriate hydration, and preventive healthcare all contribute to clearer thinking, improved concentration, and greater resilience during demanding periods. These practices should not be viewed as distractions from productivity but as investments that strengthen your ability to continue producing meaningful work over many years. **The quality of your contribution is often closely connected to the quality of the foundation supporting it.**

Mental renewal deserves equal attention. Periods of focused work should be balanced with opportunities for reflection, learning, recreation, and quiet thinking. Many creative insights emerge not while forcing solutions but while allowing the mind space to process information naturally. Walking, reading for enjoyment, spending time in nature, meaningful conversations, and thoughtful journaling all contribute to mental clarity because they create opportunities for ideas to connect in new ways. Sustainable creativity depends upon both focused effort and intentional renewal.

Emotional stewardship is another essential component of long-term success. Every professional encounters setbacks, criticism, uncertainty, and periods when progress appears slower than expected. Developing healthy emotional habits—such as patience, perspective, gratitude, resilience, and constructive self-reflection—helps prevent temporary disappointments from becoming lasting discouragement. Emotions influence decisions, and thoughtful emotional management supports wiser judgment during both success and adversity. **Resilience allows productive energy to continue flowing even when circumstances become challenging.**

Boundaries also protect valuable energy. Not every opportunity deserves acceptance. Not every request requires immediate attention. Not every meeting contributes meaningfully to your long-term mission. Learning to say no respectfully allows you to preserve time and attention for the work most closely aligned with your values and objectives. Every commitment carries an opportunity cost because accepting one responsibility often means declining another. Thoughtful boundaries help ensure that your highest energy is invested where it creates the greatest lasting value.

Regular reflection strengthens stewardship by encouraging honest evaluation of your habits. At the end of each week, ask yourself which activities produced meaningful progress and which consumed energy without corresponding benefit. Consider whether your systems remain effective, whether your priorities still reflect your purpose, and whether your schedule supports both productivity and sustainability. Small adjustments made consistently prevent unnecessary exhaustion while improving long-term effectiveness. Reflection transforms experience into continuous improvement because it encourages intentional rather than automatic living.

As you conclude this chapter's exploration of **Energy-to-Wealth Conversion**, remember that your greatest asset is not a single investment, business, product, or financial account—it is your ongoing ability to learn, create, solve problems, build relationships, and contribute meaningful value throughout your lifetime. Protect that ability carefully. Strengthen it continuously. Renew it intentionally. **When your physical, mental, emotional, and professional energy are stewarded with wisdom, they become a renewable source of lasting contribution, allowing your work to continue creating opportunities, strengthening relationships, and generating value for many years to come.**

Exercise 1: Create Your Personal Energy-to-Value System

The purpose of this exercise is to help you intentionally direct your time, attention, knowledge, and daily effort toward activities that consistently create meaningful value. Throughout this chapter, **Energy-to-Wealth Conversion** has been presented as a metaphor for transforming focused effort into skills, assets, relationships, systems, and opportunities that may produce long-term financial results. This exercise will help you identify where your energy currently goes, where it should go, and how to create a repeatable system for investing it more intentionally.

Step 1: Conduct an Energy Audit

For the next seven days, record how you spend every hour.
Group your activities into categories such as:

- Learning
- Creating
- Planning
- Administrative work
- Communication
- Recreation
- Exercise
- Family
- Sleep
- Distractions

Do not judge yourself.
Simply collect accurate information.

Step 2: Identify High-Value Activities

Review your weekly record.

Highlight the activities that directly contribute to your long-term goals.

Examples include:

- Writing
- Studying
- Product development
- Business planning
- Customer service
- Skill development
- Research
- Investment education

These become your highest-priority activities.

Step 3: Identify Energy Drains

Circle activities that consume large amounts of time without producing meaningful long-term value.

Examples might include:

- Unnecessary social media use
- Repetitive administrative work
- Excessive multitasking
- Poor organization
- Constant interruptions

Remember that recreation has value.

This exercise focuses on unnecessary energy loss rather than healthy rest.

Step 4: Define Your Three Highest Priorities

Write the three activities that deserve your greatest daily attention. For each priority, explain:

- Why it matters.
- Who benefits.
- How it contributes to your long-term mission.

Keep these priorities visible every day.

Step 5: Schedule Daily Focus Time

Choose one uninterrupted work session.
Begin with at least ten minutes.
Protect this appointment from unnecessary interruptions.
Use this time exclusively for your highest-value work.

Step 6: Build a Daily Preparation Ritual

Before beginning focused work:

- Organize your workspace.
- Gather needed materials.
- Silence unnecessary notifications.
- Review today's objective.
- Take a few moments to settle your attention.

A consistent beginning helps prepare your mind for concentrated work.

Step 7: Create a Knowledge Capture System
Choose one method for preserving valuable ideas.
Examples include:

- A notebook.
- Digital notes.
- Research journal.
- Voice recordings.
- Organized folders.

Review these notes every week.
Knowledge becomes more valuable when it is organized.

Step 8: Build a Weekly Learning Habit

Choose one subject directly related to your long-term goals.

Study it for at least thirty to sixty minutes every week.

Write one practical lesson you will immediately apply.

Learning without application produces limited long-term value.

Step 9: Protect Your Energy
Write five habits that help you maintain sustainable productivity. Examples include:

- Adequate sleep.
- Regular exercise.
- Reading.
- Time outdoors.
- Scheduled breaks.
- Healthy meals.
- Meaningful conversations.

These habits support your long-term ability to create value.

Step 10: Conduct a Weekly Reflection

Every week answer:

- What created the greatest value?
- What distracted me?
- What should I improve?
- What did I learn?
- Which habits strengthened my focus?

Reflection transforms activity into wisdom.

Step 11: Measure Long-Term Progress

At the end of every month, review:

- Skills gained.
- Assets created.
- Projects completed.
- Systems improved.
- Relationships strengthened.
- Lessons learned.

Notice how small improvements accumulate over time.

Step 12: Write Your Energy Commitment

Complete the following statement:

"I will intentionally invest my time, attention, knowledge, and effort in activities that create lasting value. I will protect my energy, strengthen my focus, continue learning, improve my systems, and serve others with excellence. Every day, I will direct my best energy toward work that reflects my highest purpose and contributes to a meaningful future."

Read this commitment before beginning your most important work each week.

Why This Exercise Matters

Every person has access to the same twenty-four hours each day, but the results those hours produce depend upon how intentionally they are invested. By auditing your time, identifying high-value activities, protecting your attention, organizing your knowledge, strengthening your habits, and reviewing your progress consistently, you create a personal system that converts focused effort into lasting value. Over time, these deliberate choices compound into stronger skills, better decisions, meaningful assets, deeper relationships, and greater opportunities. **The greatest transformation often begins not with working harder, but with directing your energy more intentionally toward creating value that continues benefiting both you and the people you serve.**

Journal Prompts

1. What does **Energy-to-Wealth Conversion** mean to me after reading this chapter, and how has it changed the way I think about creating long-term financial value?
2. Looking at how I currently spend my time and attention, which activities create the greatest long-term value, and which activities consistently reduce my productivity?
3. Which knowledge, skill, or area of expertise should I intentionally develop over the next year to increase the value I can contribute to others?
4. How can I better protect my attention from unnecessary distractions so my highest-energy hours are invested in my most meaningful work?
5. What role does purpose play in sustaining my motivation during long-term projects, and how can I reconnect with that purpose more consistently?
6. Which systems, habits, or routines currently help me direct my energy effectively, and which ones need improvement?
7. How can I better care for my physical, mental, and emotional well-being so I have the capacity to continue creating meaningful value for many years?
8. Looking back over this chapter, which principle challenged my current thinking the most, and how will I begin applying it this week?
9. Five years from now, if I consistently invest my energy in learning, creating, improving, and serving others, what kind of person do I hope to become?
10. Beginning today, what one daily habit will have the greatest positive effect on the way I invest my time, attention, knowledge, and effort toward building lasting financial value?

Closing Reflection

Throughout this chapter, you explored one of the most important principles in *Quantum Cashflow*: **every meaningful financial result begins as an investment of personal energy before it becomes a financial outcome.** Your attention, knowledge, discipline, creativity, purpose, habits, and relationships all represent valuable resources that influence the quality of the work you create and the value you contribute to others. While money may be the visible result, the invisible investments that precede it often determine whether that result becomes temporary or enduring.

You discovered that focused attention multiplies productivity, that knowledge becomes valuable only when it is applied, that purpose gives direction to discipline, and that thoughtful stewardship protects your ability to continue creating meaningful work over a lifetime. You also learned that sustainable success depends not on endless activity but on intentionally directing your best energy toward the work that matters most.

Remember that **your energy is one of your most valuable forms of capital.** Unlike financial resources, which can often be regained after they are spent, time and attention can never be recovered once they have passed. Every hour presents an opportunity to strengthen your skills, improve your systems, deepen your relationships, expand your knowledge, or create something that continues benefiting others long after today's work has ended. Choosing where that energy goes is one of the most important financial decisions you make every single day.

It is equally important to recognize that protecting your energy is part of using it wisely. Continuous learning, meaningful rest, healthy routines, thoughtful reflection, and balanced living are not obstacles to productivity—they are investments that preserve your ability to continue contributing with excellence. Lasting prosperity is strengthened when your work is supported by a life that is sustainable, purposeful, and aligned with your deepest values.

As you continue your journey through *Quantum Cashflow*, challenge yourself to ask one simple question each morning:

"Where will today's energy create the greatest long-term value?"

Allow that question to guide your priorities, your learning, your decisions, and your daily habits. Over weeks, months, and years, those intentional choices will quietly accumulate into stronger knowledge, wiser judgment, better systems, deeper relationships, meaningful assets, and expanding opportunities.

When you consistently direct your energy toward learning, creating, improving, and serving with purpose, your efforts begin compounding in ways that extend far beyond today's results. Lasting wealth is not merely the accumulation of financial resources—it is the cumulative outcome of a lifetime spent investing your best energy where it creates the greatest and most enduring value.

Chapter 10: The Final Leap—Mastering the Art of Money Creation in 10 Minutes

---

The Daily Decision That Changes Everything

Every principle explored throughout this book leads to one central conclusion: lasting financial success is not built through occasional extraordinary effort but through consistent, intentional action repeated over time. The ten-minute principle introduced in the opening chapters was never presented as a shortcut to instant wealth. Instead, it was presented as a practical framework for transforming small, focused periods of effort into meaningful long-term progress. **The true power of ten minutes lies not in the amount of time itself, but in the consistency with which that time is invested.**

The phrase **"Mastering the Art of Money Creation"** should be understood as mastering the art of creating value. Money does not appear in isolation. It is generally exchanged because someone has solved a problem, provided a useful service, created an educational resource, developed a product, improved a process, or contributed something that benefits others. Throughout this book, every strategy has pointed back to this principle. **Financial growth is strengthened when value creation becomes a daily habit rather than an occasional event.**

By this point in your journey, you have explored the importance of perception, systems, branding, trust, automation, focused attention, purposeful action, and disciplined stewardship. Individually, each principle is valuable. Together, they form a complete operating system for long-term financial development. The ten-minute practice serves as the connecting thread because it ensures these principles become habits rather than ideas left on the pages of a book. Knowledge creates the greatest benefit when it consistently influences behavior.

Many people spend years searching for the perfect opportunity while overlooking the opportunities already within their reach. They wait for ideal circumstances, unlimited resources, or complete confidence before taking meaningful action. Yet meaningful progress often begins long before conditions feel perfect. One page written today becomes part of tomorrow's book. One lesson studied today strengthens tomorrow's decision. One customer served exceptionally well today may introduce future opportunities through trust and recommendation. **Progress belongs to those who consistently begin before everything feels complete.**

The ten-minute habit also changes your relationship with overwhelming goals. Large ambitions can sometimes feel so distant that they discourage action altogether. Breaking those ambitions into small, repeatable investments of focused effort removes much of that psychological resistance. Instead of asking yourself to complete an enormous project today, you ask yourself to complete one meaningful session. Repeated often enough, those sessions quietly accumulate into books, businesses, investments, systems, professional expertise, and lasting assets. Small victories become the building blocks of extraordinary accomplishments.

Another reason this approach succeeds is that consistency builds confidence. Every completed work session provides evidence that you are capable of honoring your commitments. Confidence grows because it is supported by repeated action rather than temporary enthusiasm. Over time, your identity begins to change. You no longer see yourself as someone hoping to become productive—you become someone who consistently creates value. **Identity is strengthened through repeated behavior because actions reinforce beliefs about who you are becoming.**

This chapter represents more than the conclusion of a book. It represents the beginning of a lifelong practice. Markets will change. Technology will evolve. New industries will emerge. Economic conditions will fluctuate. Yet the habits of disciplined learning, focused attention, thoughtful planning, continuous improvement, and meaningful service remain valuable under virtually every circumstance. These principles provide stability because they strengthen your ability to adapt while continuing to create value regardless of changing conditions.

As you begin this final chapter, remember that the greatest leap is rarely dramatic. It often occurs quietly, the moment you decide that every day deserves an intentional investment in your future. Protect your ten minutes. Expand them when appropriate. Continue learning. Continue improving. Continue creating meaningful value. Continue serving others with integrity. **The final leap is not a single event—it is the decision to make purposeful action a permanent part of your daily life. When that decision becomes a habit, your capacity to create opportunity, strengthen your financial future, and build lasting prosperity continues growing long after this book has been finished.**

Building a Lifetime Value-Creation Habit

One of the greatest misconceptions about financial success is that it is achieved once and then remains unchanged forever. In reality, meaningful prosperity is sustained through habits that continue long after a specific goal has been reached. Publishing one successful book does not end the practice of writing. Launching a thriving business does not eliminate the need for innovation. Reaching a savings goal does not remove the importance of wise stewardship. **Success is not a destination where growth stops—it is an ongoing practice of creating value consistently throughout your lifetime.**

The ten-minute habit introduced in this book was never intended to be temporary. It is designed to become a permanent rhythm of intentional progress. Some days your focused session may involve learning a new skill. On other days it may involve refining a business process, strengthening customer relationships, writing new material, reviewing investments responsibly, organizing financial records, or planning future projects. The activity may change, but the commitment remains the same: invest focused attention every day in something that strengthens your future ability to create value.

Habits become powerful because they reduce the need for constant decision-making. If every productive action depends upon feeling motivated, progress naturally becomes inconsistent because motivation rises and falls. Habits create stability by establishing routines that continue regardless of temporary emotions. The question changes from **"Do I feel like working today?"** to **"What meaningful value will I create during today's focused session?"** This subtle shift transforms productivity from an emotional response into a dependable practice.

A lifetime value-creation habit also encourages continual curiosity. Every industry changes. New technologies emerge. Customer expectations evolve. Better methods are discovered. Professionals who remain committed to learning are better prepared to adapt because they view change as an opportunity for improvement rather than a threat to previous success. Curiosity keeps your knowledge relevant while allowing your work to continue meeting the changing needs of the people you serve.

Consistency does not require every day to be extraordinary. There will be seasons of rapid growth and seasons of slower progress. Some work sessions will produce major breakthroughs, while others will focus on careful refinement or routine maintenance. All of these contribute to long-term success because every meaningful improvement strengthens the foundation beneath future achievements. **Progress should be measured by faithfulness to the process rather than by the excitement of any single day.**

Another benefit of this lifelong habit is resilience. Unexpected challenges, changing markets, personal setbacks, and professional disappointments are inevitable. Individuals who maintain daily habits of learning, planning, creating, and improving often recover more effectively because they already possess systems that support continued progress. Rather than starting over completely after every difficulty, they continue building upon an existing foundation strengthened through years of consistent practice.

As your habits mature, your perspective also changes. Instead of asking whether a task produces immediate financial reward, you begin asking whether it strengthens your long-term ability to contribute meaningful value. Reading one chapter of an educational book, documenting an improved workflow, strengthening a customer relationship, refining a manuscript, or learning a new technical skill may not produce instant income. However, each investment increases your future capacity to solve problems, serve others, and recognize opportunities. **Long-term thinking transforms ordinary daily actions into valuable investments rather than isolated tasks.**

As you continue the journey beyond this book, remember that the greatest financial advantage you can develop is not one extraordinary strategy but a dependable habit of consistent value creation. Protect your daily practice. Continue strengthening your knowledge. Continue improving your systems. Continue serving others with integrity. Allow each focused session to become another investment in the person you are becoming. **When creating meaningful value becomes part of your identity rather than merely something you occasionally do, financial growth becomes the natural by-product of a life devoted to continuous learning, thoughtful contribution, and disciplined excellence.**

Thinking Like a Long-Term Wealth Architect

One of the most significant transitions in a person's financial journey occurs when they stop thinking only about earning income and begin thinking about building enduring systems. Income is important because it supports daily life, but systems create the capacity for consistent value generation over many years. A wealth architect looks beyond today's paycheck, this month's sales, or this quarter's results and begins asking a different question: **"What am I building today that will continue creating value tomorrow?"** This perspective transforms daily decisions because every action is evaluated according to its long-term contribution rather than its immediate reward.

Long-term thinking encourages the creation of assets rather than the constant exchange of time for money. Assets may include books, educational materials, intellectual property, software, investment portfolios, professional expertise, documented systems, customer relationships, or businesses that continue serving others long after the initial effort has been invested. Each asset represents stored value capable of supporting future opportunities. **The more thoughtfully you build assets, the more your previous work continues contributing to future progress.**

A wealth architect also understands the importance of designing strong foundations before pursuing rapid expansion. Buildings rely upon carefully engineered foundations because greater height requires greater stability. The same principle applies to financial life. Organized records, dependable systems, clear goals, ethical leadership, continuous learning, and disciplined habits may appear less exciting than rapid growth, yet they provide the strength necessary to support future opportunities responsibly. Growth without structure often creates unnecessary stress, while structure supports sustainable expansion.

Patience becomes one of the architect's greatest strengths. Meaningful projects frequently require years rather than weeks. Businesses mature gradually. Reputations develop through repeated experiences. Educational resources expand over time. Investment strategies often benefit from long-term discipline rather than constant adjustment. Wealth architects recognize that meaningful progress compounds because each completed project strengthens future opportunities. **Time becomes an ally when consistent effort is invested in building lasting value rather than chasing immediate results.**

Long-term thinking also influences financial decision-making. Instead of asking whether an expense is affordable today, the wealth architect asks whether it strengthens or weakens future capacity. Instead of pursuing every available opportunity, careful evaluation determines which opportunities align with the broader mission. Resources are allocated thoughtfully because every decision affects future flexibility. This approach encourages stewardship rather than impulse, allowing today's choices to support tomorrow's possibilities.

Another defining characteristic of wealth architects is documentation. Plans are written. Systems are organized. Lessons are recorded. Goals are reviewed. Processes are refined continuously. Documentation transforms experience into knowledge that remains useful long after individual projects have ended. It also creates consistency because successful practices can be repeated while mistakes become valuable teachers rather than forgotten experiences. **Written systems preserve wisdom, making future progress more efficient and intentional.**

A long-term perspective naturally encourages legacy thinking as well. Beyond financial achievement, consider what your work contributes to future generations, your professional community, your family, your readers, your customers, or your industry. Every educational resource, ethical business decision, thoughtful innovation, and meaningful relationship extends the influence of your work beyond immediate financial outcomes. Prosperity becomes more meaningful when it creates lasting benefits for others as well as personal success.

As you move toward the conclusion of *Quantum Cashflow*, remember that the most successful builders rarely measure progress only by today's results. They measure it by the quality of the foundation being constructed, the strength of the systems being developed, and the value their work will continue creating years into the future. Continue building patiently. Continue strengthening your assets. Continue refining your systems. Continue investing in knowledge, relationships, and integrity. **When you begin thinking like a long-term wealth architect, every thoughtful decision becomes another carefully placed stone in a financial structure designed not merely to survive but to continue serving, growing, and creating value for generations to come.**

Turning Every Day Into an Investment in Your Future

One of the most powerful habits you can develop is learning to view each day not simply as another period of time to complete tasks, but as an opportunity to make meaningful investments in your future. Every decision you make either strengthens or weakens the person you are becoming. Every book you read expands your knowledge. Every skill you practice increases your competence. Every relationship you nurture strengthens your network of trust. Every system you improve creates greater efficiency. Every thoughtful action contributes to the life you are intentionally building. **The greatest financial transformation often begins when you stop spending your days and start investing them.**

An investment mindset changes how ordinary activities are perceived. Learning a new technology is no longer simply studying—it is expanding your future ability to solve problems. Organizing financial records is no longer routine administration—it is strengthening your capacity for wise decision-making. Writing a chapter is no longer merely completing an assignment—it is creating an asset that may continue educating readers for years. When viewed through the lens of long-term value, even small daily actions become meaningful because they contribute to future opportunities that do not yet exist.

This perspective also encourages patience with gradual progress. Financial success is rarely built through one extraordinary day. Instead, it develops through thousands of ordinary days used intentionally. Some days produce visible accomplishments, while others focus on planning, learning, revising, or strengthening existing systems. None of these days are wasted when they contribute to your long-term mission. **Compounding depends upon consistency, and consistency depends upon respecting the value of each individual day.**

Viewing each day as an investment also encourages greater intentionality with your schedule. Rather than allowing the most urgent tasks to consume all available attention, begin protecting time for activities that strengthen your future. Schedule learning before distractions appear. Reserve uninterrupted periods for creative work. Plan regular financial reviews. Document improvements while they remain fresh in your mind. Purposeful scheduling ensures that long-term priorities receive consistent attention instead of whatever time remains after immediate responsibilities have been completed.

Reflection strengthens this investment mindset by helping you recognize the returns generated by your daily efforts. At the end of each day, ask yourself what you learned, what value you created, what relationships you strengthened, what systems you improved, and what opportunities became clearer. These questions gradually shift your attention away from simply measuring activity and toward evaluating meaningful progress. Reflection transforms experience into wisdom because it encourages learning from both success and difficulty.

Your future is also shaped by the standards you maintain today. Every decision to produce quality work, communicate honestly, honor commitments, continue learning, and improve your craft reinforces the professional identity you are developing. High standards should not become perfectionism that prevents action. Instead, they should represent a commitment to continuous excellence. **Every day you practice excellence, you strengthen the habits that make exceptional work increasingly natural.**

Gratitude provides another valuable perspective. Recognizing opportunities already available—your existing knowledge, relationships, resources, experiences, and capacity to learn—creates a foundation from which future growth becomes easier to appreciate. Gratitude does not replace ambition; rather, it balances ambition with appreciation, allowing you to pursue meaningful goals while recognizing the value of today's progress. This balanced perspective supports sustainable motivation because success is measured not only by distant achievements but also by continual growth.

As you near the conclusion of *Quantum Cashflow*, remember that your future is quietly being shaped by the choices you make today. Invest your attention intentionally. Invest your knowledge generously. Invest your effort wisely. Invest your character consistently. Invest your time where it creates lasting value. **When each day becomes a deliberate investment rather than something merely to be completed, your future begins taking shape through thousands of thoughtful decisions that gradually accumulate into a life marked by wisdom, meaningful contribution, lasting prosperity, and enduring purpose.**

The Legacy of Continuous Value Creation

Every meaningful financial journey eventually arrives at an important realization: wealth is not ultimately measured by what you accumulate but by what you continue creating and contributing throughout your lifetime. Financial resources provide opportunities, but the ability to consistently generate value is the true source of enduring prosperity. Markets rise and fall, industries evolve, technologies change, and economic conditions fluctuate. Yet the capacity to learn, adapt, solve problems, and serve others remains one of the most resilient assets you can ever possess. **Your greatest financial advantage is not what you own today—it is your continuing ability to create value tomorrow.**

Legacy begins with consistency rather than scale. Few lasting achievements begin as massive enterprises. Great libraries begin with a single book. Successful companies often begin by solving one important problem well. Educational movements frequently start with one teacher committed to helping others understand. Communities are strengthened one relationship at a time. Every enduring contribution grows because someone remained faithful to a meaningful purpose long enough for its influence to expand naturally. **Small acts of excellence repeated consistently often become the foundation of extraordinary legacies.**

A value-creating legacy also extends beyond financial measurements. Every person you mentor, every reader you educate, every customer you serve with integrity, every colleague you encourage, and every system you improve contributes to a broader impact that cannot always be measured by revenue alone. Financial success becomes far more meaningful when it supports knowledge, opportunity, innovation, and positive change in the lives of others. Lasting prosperity is strengthened when it creates benefits that continue extending beyond your immediate circumstances.

One of the defining characteristics of individuals who leave enduring legacies is their commitment to continuous improvement. They never assume they have reached the final stage of growth. Instead, they continue studying, refining their skills, improving their systems, listening carefully to feedback, and adapting thoughtfully to changing circumstances. This commitment keeps their work relevant because it evolves alongside the needs of the people they serve. **A legacy remains valuable when its creator remains committed to learning.**

Another essential principle is stewardship. Valuable work deserves careful maintenance. Books benefit from revision and updated editions. Businesses require thoughtful leadership. Investments deserve responsible oversight. Professional relationships flourish through continued communication and trust. Personal health supports long-term contribution. Stewardship recognizes that creating something meaningful is only the beginning; preserving and strengthening it requires ongoing care. Every generation of thoughtful improvement increases the lasting value of what has already been built.

Humility also protects a lasting legacy. Success should encourage gratitude rather than complacency. Every accomplishment rests upon countless opportunities, lessons, relationships, and moments of perseverance accumulated over time. Remaining teachable allows continued growth while helping you recognize that no achievement marks the end of learning. Humility invites collaboration, strengthens relationships, and keeps attention focused on meaningful contribution rather than personal recognition. **The strongest legacies are often built by people whose primary goal was serving others exceptionally well rather than becoming widely admired.**

As your work expands, remember to document your knowledge and systems for the benefit of others. Record lessons learned. Preserve successful processes. Share practical insights. Organize resources thoughtfully. Every piece of wisdom you capture today becomes a gift to your future self and potentially to those who continue building upon your work. Documentation transforms individual experience into lasting knowledge capable of serving people long after the original circumstances have passed.

As this final chapter approaches its conclusion, remember that the greatest measure of success is not whether you experienced one remarkable financial season, but whether you developed the habits, character, systems, and wisdom that allow meaningful value to continue flowing throughout your lifetime. Continue investing in learning. Continue strengthening your integrity. Continue refining your work. Continue serving others with excellence. **When your life becomes dedicated to continuous value creation, your influence extends far beyond financial achievement, leaving behind a legacy of knowledge, trust, opportunity, and meaningful contribution that continues creating value for years—and perhaps generations—to come.**

Exercise 1: Create Your Lifetime Value-Creation Blueprint

The purpose of this exercise is to help you integrate every major principle from *Quantum Cashflow* into one practical, repeatable plan that you can continue using long after finishing this book. Rather than treating financial growth as a series of isolated goals, you will design a personal blueprint built upon value creation, continuous learning, disciplined systems, thoughtful stewardship, and consistent daily action. **The objective is to leave this book with a living framework that guides your decisions for years to come.**

Step 1: Write Your Financial Vision Statement

Write a one-page description of the financial life you want to create over the next ten years.

Include questions such as:

- What kind of work do I want to be known for?
- What value will I consistently create?
- What kind of lifestyle am I building?
- What impact do I hope my work will have?
- What legacy do I want to leave?

Focus on purpose before numbers.

Step 2: Review the Principles From This Book

Create a list of the major lessons that had the greatest impact on your thinking.

Examples may include:

- Time is valuable.
- Systems create consistency.
- Trust is earned.
- Branding reflects character.
- Knowledge becomes valuable through application.
- Automation supports stewardship.
- Daily habits compound.
- Focus multiplies productivity.

Write one practical way you will apply each principle.

Step 3: Identify Your Greatest Strengths

List your strongest personal and professional assets.
Include:

- Skills
- Experience
- Knowledge
- Relationships
- Creative abilities
- Professional reputation
- Existing products or services
- Personal qualities

These strengths become the foundation of your future growth.

Step 4: Identify Your Greatest Opportunities for Improvement

Write five areas where intentional growth would significantly increase your ability to create value.

Examples include:

- Communication
- Leadership
- Financial literacy
- Technology
- Marketing
- Writing
- Public speaking
- Organization

Next to each area, write one action you will begin this month.

Step 5: Design Your Daily Ten-Minute Practice

Create a repeatable daily schedule.

Decide exactly when your ten-minute session will occur.

Write what you will focus on during those sessions.

Examples include:

- Writing
- Research
- Learning
- Planning
- Reviewing finances
- Product development
- Skill practice

Treat this appointment as non-negotiable.

Step 6: Build Your Annual Learning Plan

Choose five books, courses, certifications, or areas of study that will strengthen your expertise during the coming year.

Write:

- Why each topic matters.
- When you will study it.
- How you will apply what you learn.

Learning becomes valuable through implementation.

Step 7: Build Your Asset Development Plan

List the assets you want to create over the next five years. Examples include:

- Books
- Digital products
- Educational courses
- Businesses
- Investment accounts
- Intellectual property
- Professional systems
- Research libraries

Estimate realistic completion dates for each.

Step 8: Create Your Weekly Review Process

Once each week answer the following:

- What value did I create?
- What did I learn?
- What system improved?
- Which relationship grew stronger?
- What obstacle did I overcome?
- What deserves attention next week?

Keep these reflections together in one journal.

Step 9: Design Your Long-Term Dashboard

Choose the measurements that matter most.

Examples include:

- Assets created
- Books published
- Customers served
- Hours spent learning
- Savings growth
- Business revenue
- Systems documented
- New skills mastered

Review these indicators every month.

Step 10: Create Your Personal Standards
Write ten standards you refuse to compromise.
Examples include:

- I communicate honestly.
- I honor my commitments.
- I continue learning.
- I serve people respectfully.
- I protect my reputation.
- I produce quality work.
- I review my systems regularly.
- I improve continuously.

These standards become your decision-making guide.

Step 11: Write Your Legacy Statement

Complete the following sentence:

"When people remember my work, I hope they remember that I consistently created meaningful value by living with integrity, pursuing excellence, serving generously, continuing to learn, and leaving every project stronger than I found it."

Read this statement every month to keep your long-term purpose clear.

Step 12: Write Your Lifetime Commitment

Complete the following declaration:

"I understand that lasting prosperity is created through consistent value creation, disciplined habits, thoughtful systems, continuous learning, ethical leadership, and meaningful service. I will invest my time intentionally, strengthen my knowledge continually, improve my work consistently, and build assets that benefit others for many years to come. Every day, I will choose progress over procrastination, stewardship over waste, excellence over convenience, and purpose over distraction. My financial future will be shaped not by isolated moments of inspiration but by the steady accumulation of wise decisions repeated throughout my lifetime."

Sign and date this commitment.

Review it at the beginning of every year as a reminder that your greatest investment will always be the person you continue becoming.

Why This Exercise Matters

Books create their greatest value when their ideas become daily practice. This exercise transforms the principles of *Quantum Cashflow* into a practical operating system for lifelong financial growth. By clarifying your vision, strengthening your habits, building valuable assets, measuring meaningful progress, and committing yourself to continuous improvement, you move beyond temporary motivation and into intentional action. **True financial mastery is not achieved through one extraordinary opportunity—it is built through thousands of thoughtful decisions that consistently transform your time, knowledge, character, and effort into lasting value for both yourself and the people you serve.**

Journal Prompts

1. Looking back over *Quantum Cashflow*, which principle has had the greatest impact on my thinking, and why do I believe it will influence my future decisions?
2. How has my understanding of wealth changed from focusing primarily on earning money to focusing on consistently creating meaningful value?
3. Which daily habit introduced in this book has the greatest potential to improve my life over the next five years if I practice it consistently?
4. What strengths have I discovered within myself while working through these chapters, and how can I continue developing them?
5. Which areas of my personal or professional life still require the greatest improvement, and what specific actions will I begin taking immediately?
6. How do I want my work, leadership, business, or creative contributions to positively influence the people I serve over the coming decades?
7. Looking ten years into the future, what kinds of assets, knowledge, systems, relationships, and accomplishments would make me feel that I invested my time wisely?
8. Which limiting habits, distractions, or outdated beliefs am I prepared to leave behind as I continue building a life centered on continuous value creation?
9. If I wrote a letter to my future self twenty years from now, what advice, encouragement, and commitments would I include to ensure I remained faithful to the principles explored throughout this book?
10. Beginning today, what one decision will symbolize my commitment to making value creation, lifelong learning, disciplined ac-

tion, thoughtful stewardship, and meaningful contribution permanent parts of my daily life?

Closing Reflection

You have now reached the final pages of *Quantum Cashflow*, but in many ways, your most important work is only beginning.

Throughout this journey, one central principle has quietly connected every chapter: **lasting financial growth is most sustainably built through the consistent creation of meaningful value.** Every discussion about time, focused attention, disciplined habits, trust, branding, systems, automation, learning, stewardship, and purpose ultimately pointed toward the same enduring truth. Financial opportunity grows strongest when individuals continually develop their ability to solve problems, improve lives, strengthen relationships, and contribute work that remains useful long after it has been completed.

The ten-minute practice introduced at the beginning of this book was never presented as a shortcut or a promise of instant wealth. Instead, it serves as a reminder that remarkable achievements often begin with small, intentional actions repeated consistently over time. A single focused work session may appear modest in isolation, yet hundreds of such sessions accumulate into books, businesses, professional expertise, improved systems, stronger relationships, organized finances, valuable assets, and opportunities that once seemed impossible. **Consistency transforms ordinary effort into extraordinary outcomes because time allows disciplined actions to compound.**

Remember that your greatest financial asset is not found in a bank account, an investment portfolio, or a business alone. Your greatest asset is your continuing ability to learn, adapt, think critically, communicate effectively, build trust, solve meaningful problems, and create value that others genuinely appreciate. Markets may change, industries may evolve, and technologies will continue advancing, but these qualities remain valuable because they strengthen your ability to contribute under changing circumstances.

As you move forward, continue protecting your attention, refining your systems, expanding your knowledge, strengthening your character, and investing intentionally in the habits that support long-term growth.

Continue asking thoughtful questions. Continue improving one small process at a time. Continue building assets that serve people well. Continue treating your reputation as one of your most valuable investments. Above all, continue measuring success not only by financial results but also by the quality of the contribution your work makes to the lives of others.

There will be seasons of rapid progress and seasons of slower growth. There will be unexpected opportunities and unavoidable challenges. During each season, return to the principles that guided this book: learn continuously, act consistently, improve patiently, communicate honestly, serve generously, and build thoughtfully. These practices create resilience because they strengthen the person behind the financial results rather than depending upon circumstances alone.

As you close this book, remember that every new day offers another opportunity to invest ten intentional minutes in becoming a wiser learner, a stronger creator, a more thoughtful leader, and a more disciplined steward of your resources. Those ten minutes may eventually become thirty, an hour, or an entire career devoted to meaningful contribution—but the habit always begins with one intentional decision.

Your financial future will not be defined by a single breakthrough or one extraordinary moment. It will be shaped by the countless choices you make to learn, create, improve, and serve with integrity every day. Continue building patiently, continue creating value faithfully, and continue investing your time where it has the greatest potential to strengthen both your life and the lives of others. That is the enduring foundation of sustainable prosperity, and it is a journey that can continue for the rest of your lifetime.

Appendix A: The Wealth Reality Shift Exercise

The purpose of this exercise is to help you intentionally shift your attention from merely earning money to consistently creating meaningful value. Throughout *Quantum Cashflow*, you have learned that sustainable financial growth is strengthened through disciplined habits, focused attention, continuous learning, thoughtful systems, and purposeful action. These twelve simple steps are designed to help you reinforce those principles through daily reflection and consistent implementation.

Step 1

Write one clear financial goal that you are committed to pursuing over the next twelve months.

Step 2

Identify one meaningful problem you can help solve for other people through your knowledge, skills, products, or services.

Step 3

List three existing strengths that increase your ability to create long-term value.

Step 4

Choose one high-value activity you will dedicate at least ten focused minutes to every day.

Step 5

Write one habit that consistently distracts you from your long-term financial objectives and commit to reducing its influence.

Step 6

Identify one new skill you will begin learning this month to increase the value you can provide.

Step 7

Write one practical asset you will begin creating that can continue providing value long after it is completed.

Step 8

Describe one system you can improve or simplify to make your work more efficient and consistent.

Step 9

Identify one professional relationship you will intentionally strengthen through honesty, reliability, and thoughtful communication.

Step 10

Write one daily reminder that encourages you to focus on creating value before expecting financial results.

Step 11

Record one meaningful improvement you made this week that will continue benefiting your future work.

Step 12

Finish by writing one commitment describing the person you choose to become through consistent learning, disciplined action, purposeful service, and lifelong value creation.

The 10-Minute Blueprint Journal Prompts for Infinite Income

1. If I invested ten focused minutes every day for the next year, what meaningful accomplishment would have the greatest positive impact on my future?
2. What problem can I begin solving today that would genuinely improve someone else's life?
3. Which knowledge or skill has the greatest potential to increase the value I create over the next five years?
4. What daily distraction consumes the most valuable part of my attention, and how can I replace it with purposeful action?
5. Which asset can I begin creating today that may continue generating value for years to come?
6. What does financial freedom personally mean to me beyond simply earning more money?
7. Which habit consistently moves me closer to my long-term financial vision, and how can I strengthen it?
8. How can I better organize my time so that my highest-energy hours are devoted to my highest-value work?
9. What systems can I build that would make creating value easier, more consistent, and more sustainable?
10. How can I improve my professional reputation through greater reliability, honesty, and excellence?
11. Which book, course, mentor, or educational resource should I study next to strengthen my expertise?
12. What opportunities already exist around me that I may have been overlooking?
13. How can I create more value for my current customers, readers, clients, or community?
14. What does my ideal daily routine look like if it consistently supports learning, creating, improving, and serving?

15. Which long-term project deserves ten uninterrupted minutes of focused attention today?
16. What personal belief about money, success, or opportunity no longer serves my future growth?
17. How can I better measure progress by the value I create instead of only by financial outcomes?
18. What one improvement can I make this week that my future self will appreciate one year from now?
19. If I continued practicing the principles in this book for the next decade, what kind of person would I become?
20. What is the single most important action I will take immediately after closing this book to begin turning these principles into life-long habits?

Closing Reflection

Every meaningful journey begins with a single intentional decision. Throughout *Quantum Cashflow*, you have explored practical principles centered on creating value, developing disciplined habits, strengthening systems, building trust, protecting your attention, and investing consistently in your personal and professional growth. Appendix A is designed to help transform those ideas into daily practice because knowledge becomes most valuable when it influences the way we live, think, and act.

The **Wealth Reality Shift Exercise** reminds us that financial growth begins long before money changes hands. It begins with the choices we make about how we spend our time, where we direct our attention, what skills we develop, how we serve others, and the habits we repeat every day. Small improvements often seem insignificant in the moment, yet they accumulate quietly into stronger character, greater competence, better opportunities, and a more resilient financial future.

The **10-Minute Blueprint Journal Prompts** encourage ongoing reflection because meaningful progress is rarely accidental. Reflection transforms experience into wisdom. It helps you recognize patterns, celebrate growth, adjust your direction when necessary, and remain connected to the purpose behind your work. By asking thoughtful questions regularly, you develop greater clarity about the person you are becoming and the legacy you are intentionally building.

Remember that sustainable prosperity is not defined solely by financial measurements. It is reflected in your ability to continue learning, adapting, solving problems, strengthening relationships, honoring your commitments, and creating work that genuinely improves the lives of others. Financial success becomes more meaningful when it grows alongside integrity, wisdom, generosity, and lifelong curiosity.

There will be days when progress feels obvious and rewarding, and there will be days when growth seems slow or difficult to recognize. During both seasons, return to the habits that have guided this book. Continue protecting your focused time. Continue learning with intention. Continue refining your systems. Continue strengthening your reputation. Continue creating value one thoughtful decision at a time. The consistency of these daily investments often becomes far more important than the intensity of any single effort.

As you move beyond the pages of this book, remember that your future is not determined by one extraordinary opportunity but by the cumulative effect of ordinary choices made with extraordinary consistency. Every page you write, every lesson you learn, every relationship you strengthen, every system you improve, and every problem you help solve becomes another investment in a future built on purpose and contribution.

May these exercises serve not as the conclusion of your journey, but as the beginning of a lifelong practice of intentional growth. Continue investing your time wisely, creating meaningful value, serving others with integrity, and learning without ceasing. When you make those commitments part of your daily life, you build something far more valuable than financial success alone—you build a life of enduring purpose, lasting contribution, and sustainable prosperity.

<u>**Message from the Author:**</u>

I hope you enjoyed this book, I love astrology and knew there was not a book such as this out on the shelf. I love metaphysical items as well. Please check out my other books:

-Life of Government Benefits

-My life of Hell

-My life with Hydrocephalus

-Red Sky

-World Domination:Woman's rule

-World Domination:Woman's Rule 2: The War

-Life and Banishment of Apophis: book 1

-The Kidney Friendly Diet

-The Ultimate Hemp Cookbook

-Creating a Dispensary(legally)

-Cleanliness throughout life: the importance of showering from childhood to adulthood.

-Strong Roots: The Risks of Overcoddling children

-Hemp Horoscopes: Cosmic Insights and Earthly Healing

- Celestial Hemp Navigating the Zodiac: Through the Green Cosmos

-Astrological Hemp: Aligning The Stars with Earth's Ancient Herb

-The Astrological Guide to Hemp: Stars, Signs, and Sacred Leaves

-Green Growth: Innovative Marketing Strategies for your Hemp Products and Dispensary

-Cosmic Cannabis

-Astrological Munchies

-Henry The Hemp

-Zodiacal Roots: The Astrological Soul Of Hemp

- **Green Constellations: Intersection of Hemp and Zodiac**

-Hemp in The Houses: An astrological Adventure Through The Cannabis Galaxy

-Galactic Ganja Guide

Heavenly Hemp

Zodiac Leaves
Doctor Who Astrology
Cannastrology
Stellar Satvias and Cosmic Indicas
Celestial Cannabis: A Zodiac Journey
AstroHerbology: The Sky and The Soil: Volume 1
AstroHerbology:Celestial Cannabis:Volume 2
Cosmic Cannabis Cultivation
The Starry Guide to Herbal Harmony: Volume 1
The Starry Guide to Herbal Harmony: Cannabis Universe: Volume 2
Yugioh Astrology: Astrological Guide to Deck, Duels and more
Nightmare Mansion: Echoes of The Abyss
Nightmare Mansion 2: Legacy of Shadows
Nightmare Mansion 3: Shadows of the Forgotten
Nightmare Mansion 4: Echoes of the Damned
The Life and Banishment of Apophis: Book 2
Nightmare Mansion: Halls of Despair
Healing with Herb: Cannabis and Hydrocephalus
Planetary Pot: Aligning with Astrological Herbs: Volume 1
Fast Track to Freedom: 30 Days to Financial Independence Using AI, Assets, and Agile Hustles
Cosmic Hemp Pathways
How to Become Financially Free in 30 Days: 10,000 Paths to Prosperity
Zodiacal Herbage: Astrological Insights: Volume 1
Nightmare Mansion: Whispers in the Walls
The Daleks Invade Atlantis
Henry the hemp and Hydrocephalus

10X The Kidney Friendly Diet
Cannabis Universe: Adult coloring book
Hemp Astrology: The Healing Power of the Stars

Zodiacal Herbage: Astrological Insights: Cannabis Universe: Volume 2

Planetary Pot: Aligning with Astrological Herbs: Cannabis Universes: Volume 2

Doctor Who: Convergence Protocol – The Replicator War

Nightmare Mansion: Curse of the Blood Moon

The Celestial Stoner: A Guide to the Zodiac

Cosmic Pleasures: Sex Toy Astrology for Every Sign

Hydrocephalus Astrology: Navigating the Stars and Healing Waters

Lapis and the Mischievous Chocolate Bar

Celestial Positions: Sexual Astrology for Every Sign

Apophis's Shadow Work Journal: **:** A Journey of Self-Discovery and Healing

Kinky Cosmos: Sexual Kink Astrology for Every Sign

Digital Cosmos: The Astrological Digimon Compendium

Stellar Seeds: The Cosmic Guide to Growing with Astrology

Apophis's Daily Gratitude Journal

Cat Astrology: Feline Mysteries of the Cosmos

The Cosmic Kama Sutra: An Astrological Guide to Sexual Positions

Unleash Your Potential: A Guided Journal Powered by AI Insights

Whispers of the Enchanted Grove

Cosmic Pleasures: An Astrological Guide to Sexual Kinks

369, 12 Manifestation Journal

Whisper of the nocturne journal(blank journal for writing or drawing)

The Boogey Book

Locked In Reflection: A Chastity Journey Through Locktober

Generating Wealth Quickly:How to Generate $100,000 in 24 Hours

Star Magic: Harness the Power of the Universe

The Flatulence Chronicles: A Fart Journal for Self-Discovery

The Doctor and The Death Moth

Seize the Day: A Personal Seizure Tracking Journal

The Ultimate Boogeyman Safari: A Journey into the Boogie World and Beyond

Whispers of Samhain: 1,000 Spells of Love, Luck, and Lunar Magic: Samhain Spell Book

Apophis's guides:Witch's Spellbook Crafting Guide for Halloween

Frost & Flame: The Enchanted Yule Grimoire of 1000 Winter Spells

The Ultimate Boogey Goo Guide & Spooky Activities for Halloween Fun

Harmony of the Scales: A Libra's Spellcraft for Balance and Beauty

The Enchanted Advent: 36 Days of Christmas Wonders

Nightmare Mansion: The Labyrinth of Screams

Harvest of Enchantment: 1,000 Spells of Gratitude, Love, and Fortune for Thanksgiving

The Boogey Chronicles: A Journal of Nightly Encounters and Shadowy Secrets

The 12 Days of Financial Freedom: A Step-by-Step Christmas Countdown to Transform Your Finances

Sigil of the Eternal Spiral Blank Journal

A Christmas Feast: Timeless Recipes for Every Meal

Holiday Stress-Free Solutions: A Survival Guide to Thriving During the Festive Season

Yu-Gi-Oh! Holiday Gifting Mastery: The Ultimate Guide for Fans and Newcomers Alike

Holiday Harmony: A Hydrocephalus Survival Guide for the Festive Season

Celestial Craft: The Witch's Almanac for 2025 – A Cosmic Guide to Manifestations, Moons, and Mystical Events

Doctor Who: The Toymaker's Winter Wonderland

Tulsa King Unveiled: A Thrilling Guide to Stallone's Mafia Masterpiece

Pendulum Craft: A Complete Guide to Crafting and Using Personalized Divination Tools

Nightmare Mansion: Santa's Eternal Eve

Starlight Noel: A Cosmic Journey through Christmas Mysteries

The Dark Architect: Unlocking the Blueprint of Existence

Surviving the Embrace: The Ultimate Guide to Encounters with The Hugging Molly

The Enchanted Codex: Secrets of the Craft for Witches, Wiccans, and Pagans

Harvest of Gratitude: A Complete Thanksgiving Guide

Yuletide Essentials: A Complete Guide to an Authentic and Magical Christmas

Celestial Smokes: A Cosmic Guide to Cigars and Astrology

Living in Balance: A Comprehensive Survival Guide to Thriving with Diabetes Insipidus

Cosmic Symbiosis: The Venom Zodiac Chronicles

The Cursed Paw of Ambition

Cosmic Symbiosis: The Astrological Venom Journal

Celestial Wonders Unfold: A Stargazer's Guide to the Cosmos (2024-2029)

The Ultimate Black Friday Prepper's Guide: Mastering Shopping Strategies and Savings

Cosmic Sales: The Astrological Guide to Black Friday Shopping

Legends of the Corn Mother and Other Harvest Myths

Whispers of the Harvest: The Corn Mother's Journal

The Evergreen Spellbook

The Doctor Meets the Boogeyman

The White Witch of Rose Hall's SpellBook

The Gingerbread Golem's Shadow: A Study in Sweet Darkness

The Gingerbread Golem Codex: An Academic Exploration of Sweet Myths

The Gingerbread Golem Grimoire: Sweet Magicks and Spells for the Festive Witch

The Curse of the Gingerbread Golem

10-minute Christmas Crafts for kids

Christmas Crisis Solutions: The Ultimate Last-Minute Survival Guide

Gingerbread Golem Recipes: Holiday Treats with a Magical Twist

The Infinite Key: Unlocking Mystical Secrets of the Ages

Enchanted Yule: A Wiccan and Pagan Guide to a Magical and Memorable Season

Dinosaurs of Power: Unlocking Ancient Magick

Astro-Dinos: The Cosmic Guide to Prehistoric Wisdom

Gallifrey's Yule Logs: A Festive Doctor Who Cookbook

The Dino Grimoire: Secrets of Prehistoric Magick

The Gift They Never Knew They Needed

The Gingerbread Golem's Culinary Alchemy: Enchanting Recipes for a Sweetly Dark Feast

A Time Lord Christmas: Holiday Adventures with the Doctor

Krampusproofing Your Home: Defensive Strategies for Yule

Silent Frights: A Collection of Christmas Creepypastas to Chill Your Bones

Santa Raptor's Jolly Carnage: A Dino-Claus Christmas Tale

Prehistoric Palettes: A Dino Wicca Coloring Journey

The Christmas Wishkeeper Chronicles

The Starlight Sleigh: A Holiday Journey

Elf Secrets: The True Magic of the North Pole

Candy Cane Conjurations

Cooking with Kids: Recipes Under 20 Minutes

Doctor Who: The TARDIS Confiscation

The Anxiety First Aid Kit: Quick Tools to Calm Your Mind

Frosty Whispers: A Winter's Tale

The Infinite Key: Unlocking the Secrets to Prosperity, Resilience, and Purpose

The Grasping Void: Why You'll Regret This Purchase

Astrology for Busy Bees: Star Signs Simplified

The Instant Focus Formula: Cut Through the Noise

The Secret Language of Colors: Unlocking the Emotional Codes

Sacred Fossil Chronicles: Blank Journal

The Christmas Cottage Miracle

Feeding Frenzy: Graboid-Inspired Recipes

Manifest in Minutes: The Quick Law of Attraction Guide

The Symbiote Chronicles: Doctor Who's Venomous Journey

Think Tiny, Grow Big: The Minimalist Mindset

The Energy Key: Unlocking Limitless Motivation

New Year, New Magic: Manifesting Your Best Year Yet

Unstoppable You: Mastering Confidence in Minutes

Infinite Energy: The Secret to Never Feeling Drained

Lightning Focus: Mastering the Art of Productivity in a Distracted World

Saturnalia Manifestation Magick: A Guide to Unlocking Abundance During the Solstice

Graboids and Garland: The Ultimate Tremors-Themed Christmas Guide

12 Nights of Holiday Magic

The Power of Pause: 60-Second Mindfulness Practices

The Quick Reset: How to Reclaim Your Life After Burnout

The Shadow Eater: A Tale of Despair and Survival

The Micro-Mastery Method: Transform Your Skills in Just Minutes a Day

Reclaiming Time: How to Live More by Doing Less

Chronovore: The Eternal Nexus

The Mind Reset: Unlocking Your Inner Peace in a Chaotic World

Confidence Code: Building Unshakable Self-Belief

Baby the Vampire Terrier
Baby the Vampire Terrier's Christmas Adventure
Celestial Streams: The Content Creator's Astrology Manual
The Wealth Whisperer: Unlocking Abundance with Everyday Actions
The Energy Equation: Maximize Your Output Without Burning Out
The Happiness Algorithm: Science-Backed Steps to Joyful Living
Stress-Free Success: Achieving Goals Without Anxiety
Mindful Wealth: The New Blueprint for Financial Freedom
The Festive Flavors of New Year: A Culinary Celebration
The Master's Gambit: Keys of Eternal Power
Shadowed Secrets: Groundhog Day Mysteries
Beneath the Burrow: Lessons from the Groundhog
Spring's Whispers: The Groundhog's Prediction
The Limitless Mindset: Unlock Your Untapped Potential
The Focus Funnel: How to Cut Through Chaos and Get Results
Bold Moves: Building Courage to Live on Your Terms
The Daily Shift: Simple Practices for Lasting Transformation
The Quarter-Life Reset: Thriving in Your 20s and 30s
The Art of Shadowplay: Building Your Own Personal Myth
The Eternal Loop: Finding Purpose in Repetition
Burrowing Wisdom: Life Lessons from the Groundhog
Shadow Work: A Groundhog Day Perspective
Love in Bloom: 5-Minute Romantic Gestures
The Shadowspell Codex: Secrets of Forbidden Magick
The Burnout Cure: Finding Balance in a Busy World
The Groundhog Prophecy: Unlocking Seasonal Secrets
Nog Tales: The Spirited History of Eggnog
Six More Weeks: Embracing Seasonal Transitions
The Lumivian Chronicles: Fragments of the Fifth Dimension
Money on Your Mind: A Beginner's Guide to Wealth
The Focus Fix: Breaking Through Distraction

January's Spirit Keepers: Mystical Protectors of the Cold
Creativity Unchained: Unlocking Your Wildest Ideas in 2025
Manifestation Mastery: 365 Days to Rewrite Your Reality
The Groundhog's Mirror: Reflecting on Change
The Weeping Angels' Christmas Curse
Burrowed in Time: A Groundhog Day Journey
Heartbeats: Poems to Share with Your Valentine
Dino Wicca: The Sacred Grimoire of Prehistoric Magick
Courage of the Pride: Finding Your Inner Roar
The Lion's Leap: Bold Moves for Big Results
Healthy Hustle: Achieving Without Overworking
Practical Manifesting: Turning Dreams into Reality in 2025
Jurassic Pharaohs: Unlocking the Magick of Ancient Egypt and Dino Wicca
The Happiness Equation: Small Changes for Big Joy
The Confidence Compass: Finding Your Inner Strength
Whispers in the Hollow: Tales of the Forgotten Beasts
Echoes from the Hollow: The Return of Forgotten Beasts
The Hollow Ascendant: The Rise of the Forgotten Beasts
The Relationship Reset: Building Better Connections
Mastering the Morning: How to Win the Day Before 8 AM
The Shadow's Dance: Groundhog Day Symbolism
Cupid's Kitchen: Quick Valentine's Day Recipes
Valentine's Day on a Budget: Love Without Breaking the Bank
Astrocraft: Aligning the Stars in the World of Minecraft
Forecasting Life: Groundhog Day Reflections
Bleeding Hearts: Twisted Tales of Valentine's Terror
Herbal Smoke Revolution: The Ultimate Guide to Nature's Cigarette Alternative
Winter's Wrath: The Complete Survival Blueprint for Extreme Freezes.
The Groundhog's Shadow: A Tale of Seasons
Burrowed Insights: Wisdom from the Groundhog

Sensual Strings: The Art of Erotic Bondage
Whispered Flames: Unlocking the Power of Fire Play
Forgotten Shadows: A Guide to Cryptids Lost to Time
Six Weeks of Secrets: Groundhog Day's Hidden Messages
Shadows and Cycles: Groundhog Day Reflections
The Art of Love Letters: Crafting the Perfect Message
Romantic Getaways at Home: Turning Your Space into Paradise
Purrfect Brews: A Cat Lover's Guide to Coffee and Companionship
The Groundhog's Wisdom: Timeless Lessons for Modern Life
The Shadow Oracle: Groundhog Day as a Predictor
Emerging from the Burrow: A Journey of Renewal
The Language of Love: Learning Your Partner's Love Style
Authorpreneur: The Ultimate Blueprint for Writing, Publishing, and Thriving as an Author
Weathering the Seasons: Groundhog Day Perspectives
Valentine's Day Magic: A Guide to Romantic Rituals
The Shadow Chronicles: Stories of Groundhog Day
Love and Laughter: Fun Games for Valentine's Day
AstroRealty: Unlocking the Stars for Property Success
The Groundhog's Path: A Guide to Seasonal Balance
Groundhog Day Diaries: Reflections in the Shadow
The Groundhog's Light: Illuminating the Path Ahead
Valentine's Traditions from Around the World
AI Wealth Revolution: Unlocking the Trillionaire Mindset
Love Rekindled: Reigniting Passion in Relationships
Single and Thriving: Self-Love on Valentine's Day
Emerald Legends: Mystical Tales of Ireland
Green Alchemy: Harnessing Nature's Magic
The Hearts of Horror: A Valentine's Day Nightmare
The Leprechaun's Guide to Wealth and Wisdom
Dancing with the Sidhe: Celebrating the Otherworld

Shamrocks and Shadows: Mysteries of the Green Isle

Emerald Energy: Harnessing Luck and Growth

The Gingerbread Golem's Valentine: A Sweetheart's Guide to Love and Enchantment

The Celtic Knot: Weaving Life and Destiny

Green Fire: Elemental Magic for St. Patrick's Day

Clover Chronicles: Finding Your Inner Luck

Ireland's Mystical Creatures: A Field Guide

Gingerbread Golem's Love Almanac

Prowl and Thrive: The Lion's Guide to Success

Love Alchemy: Transforming Your Life Through Heart Energy

WORLD DOMINATION: Woman's Rule 3:The New Life

The Midnight Rose: A Guide to Lunar Love Spells

The Forbidden Letters: Writing Your Own Love Prophecy

Luck and Lore: St. Patrick's Day for Modern Mystics

The Green Path: A Pagan Celebration of Renewal

The Dark Architect's Guide to Reprogramming Reality

Prankster's Paradise: A Guide to Harmless Hijinks

Manifest Your Reality: The Law of Attraction Simplified

The TARDIS Owner's Manual: Understanding the Doctor's Ship: *A complete guide to the TARDIS, its technology, secrets, and mysteries*

Starlit Romance: Astrology Secrets for Finding True Love

The Time Lord's Atlas: A Complete Guide to the Whoniverse: ***A breakdown of the locations, planets, and dimensions explored in Doctor Who***

Sweetheart Shadows: The Dark Side of Love and Attraction

February Fire: Reigniting Passion in Every Area of Life

The Self-Love Toolkit: 5 Ways to Embrace Who You Are

February Sparks: Ignite Your Dreams in 28 Days

March to Success: A 31-Day Action Blueprint

Ancient Paths: The 13 Sacred Principles of Dino Wicca

Echoes of Tomorrow: Navigating the AI Revolution
The Wellness Blueprint: Balancing Mind, Body, and Soul
Green Horizons: Sustainable Living for a Better Tomorrow
The AI Wealth Code: How to Make Millions with Automation
AI-Powered Creativity: Writing, Art, and Music for Profit
Extinction Rites: Rebirthing Your Soul Through Prehistoric Magick
Sacred Serpents tarot
Celestial Enchantment blank journal
Star Strains
Culinary Journeys: Exploring Global Flavors at Home
The Hollowvale Curse
The Hollowvale Harvest
The Egg of Transformation: Awakening Your Inner Power
Blooming Into Power: A Wiccan Guide to Spring Awakening
The Nightmare Nexus: The Third Doctor's Perilous Haunting
Digital Detox: Reclaiming Your Life in a Connected World
Ostara's Path: Walking the Spiral of Renewal
The Sacred Hare
Financial Freedom: Building Wealth in the Modern Age
Spring's Cauldron: Stirring the Waters of Change
The Hollowvale Pact
Quantum Consciousness: The Science of Reality Shifting
The Hollowvale Hunger
The Sacred Waters Within: A Witch's Guide to Hydrocephalus Magick
The Raven's Nest: Building a Life of Unshakable Stability
AI and the Human Mind: The Future of Intelligence
The Hollowvale Reckoning
Timeless Love: Building and Maintaining Lasting Relationships
The Raven's Roar: Unlocking Unstoppable Confidence
Raven Sight: Awakening Intuition and Inner Wisdom

The Butterfly Effect: Small Changes, Big Transformations
Taming the Boogeyman: How to Conquer Your Inner Fears
The Magick of Green: Awakening Earth's Energy in You
The Entrepreneurial Mindset: Secrets to Business Success
The Hollowvale End
The Shadow Luck Ritual: Reclaiming Power from Your Dark Side
Spring Magick for Beginners: A Simple Guide to Seasonal Energy Work
Doctor Who: The Hollowvale Conundrum
The March of Miracles: Unlocking Synchronicities in Spring
Unveiling the Cosmos: A Guide to Stargazing and Space Exploration
The Ultimate Guide to Surviving an Economic Collapse
The AI Gold Rush: How to Profit from the AI Revolution
Bastet's Shadow: The Hidden Power of Feline Magick
The Bastet Codex: Unlocking the Goddess's Magickal Secrets
Purring Spells: Harnessing Bastet's Healing Frequencies
Bastet's Nine Lives: Rebirth, Transformation, and Immortality Spells
Primal Currents: Hydrocephalus Magick in the Path of Dino Wicca
The Digital Gold Rush: Mastering E-Commerce and Online Sales
Future Shock: Adapting to the Next Decade of Change
The Quantum Mindset: Think Like a Billionaire
Sacred Motherhood: Awakening the Divine Feminine Within
The Mother's Spellbook: Enchantments for Love, Protection, and Prosperity
The Witch's Guide to Parenting: Raising Empowered and Intuitive Children
The Magick of Motherhood: Reclaiming Your Power Through Rituals

The Pagan Path to Self-Love: A Goddess's Guide to Worth and Confidence
Wild Woman Magick: Unleashing Your Primal Power
The Money Magnet Blueprint: Unlocking Unlimited Wealth
Biohacking 101: Unlock Your Body's Full Potential
The Wild Father: A Pagan Guide to Strength and Wisdom
The Sacred Masculine: Unlocking Your Inner Power
The Druid's Compass
The Warrior's Mindset
The Father's Fire
Odin's Path
Ancestral Bonds
The House That Whispers
The Magician's Code
The Wild Hunt
The Green Man's Path
The Altar of Success
The Shadow and the Sword
The High Priestess's Guide to Energy Healing
The Lunar Mother
The Sacred Self-Care Grimoire
The Womb Wisdom Codex
The Wheel of the Mother
The Witch's Guide to Manifestation
The Q2 Reset
The Ultimate Guide to AI-Powered Passive Income
Escape the 9-5
AI Feline Fortunes
The Tear-Stained Grimoire
Razorblade Runes
Cemetery Sirens
The Midnight Wristwatch
The Town That Forgets

AI Horror & Creepypasta
The Hollow Frequency
The Breach Echo
The Quiet Between Worlds
The Sigil of Tharan-Khul
Summon the Vault of Y'ha'ten
The Becoming Codex
The Profit of Az'ra-nar
The Drowned Logos
Echoes of the Eldritch Will
The Deep Ledger
Necronomicon of Networth
Covenant of the Wealthwyrm
The Whisperer's Manifesto
The Rites of Azh-K'luth
The Ark of the Crawling Coin
The Tithe of Shadows
Inkheart Abyss
The Timewinds of Y'ha-nthlei
The Spiral Labyrinth of Azag-Nirrh
The Gallifreyan Heresy of the Black Pharaoh
The Psalms of Nyog-Sotha
Black Rain Alchemy
The Infinite Maw
The Entropic Blueprint
The Oracle of Sh'guul
The Book of Breach
The Drowned Saint's Testament
Dreamcraft of the Sleeper God
The Silence Market
Cthonomics: The Dark Wealth Algorithm
Invocation of the Ten-Eyed King
Wealthbound to the Wyrm Below

Become the Unnameable
Codex of the Sovereign Flame
Rituals of Relentless Becoming
The Shadow Ascends
The Eyes Beneath You
The Will That Wakes Worlds
Silence Is a Weapon
The Mirror That Screams
The Whisper Between Moments
The Mind That Devours Fear
The Myth of the Finished Self
The Architect of Your Madness
The Voice You've Buried
The Discipline of Madness
Stormborn: Awakening Your Inner Tempest
The Mind That Ate Time
Unbind Your Becoming
The Pact You Owe Yourself
The Devourer's Diet
The Acid That Carves the Path
The Tower You Must Burn
The Breath Between Worlds
Speak Like the Deep
The Labyrinth Within
The Spine of the Sea God
Rejection Is a Portal
The Crown You Refused
The Scar Is the Spell
The Lightless Flame
The Habit of Becoming Horrific
ChickenJockey Chaos
The Gatekeeper Within
You Are Not Your Name

The Compass of the Mad
The Archive of Unsent Letters
What the Mirror Can't Show You
The Knife You Needed
Worship Nothing, Become Everything
The Other Voice
The Body the World Forgot
The Vein of the Void
The Black Bone Codex
The Puzzle of the Hidden Self (Millennium Puzzle)
The Eye That Sees the Lie *(Millennium Eye)*
The Ring of Return (Millennium Ring)
The Rod of Relentless Will ***(Millennium Rod)***
The Tally of the Soul (Millennium Tauk/Necklace)
The Key to the Locked Timeline (Millennium Key)
The Scale of Sacred Decisions (Millennium Scales)
Inferno Bites: The UnOfficial Minecraft Lava Cookbook
Rot in the Attic
Prana: The Hidden Force of Your Infinite Self
The Shadow Realm Within: Transforming Darkness Into Destiny
The Borderland Collapse
Claws of Protection: Bastet's Defensive Magick
Mr. Ring-a-Ding's Madness
Yugioh Astrology: Celestial Deckcraft and Duel Destiny (2026–2027 Edition)
The Seal You Signed: Unlocking the Power You Once Feared
The Puzzle of Infinite Minds: Unlocking the Mentalism Hidden Within
The Eye That Mirrors the All: Secrets of Inner Reflection
Doctor Who: The Toymaker's Broadcast
The Rod of Eternal Flow: Commanding the Currents of Vibration

Golden Eyes of Bastet: Enhancing Psychic Vision
The Key of Dual Forces: Balance Within the Polarity
The Scales of Living Rhythm: Timing the Dance of Life
The Necklace of Hidden Cause: Weaving the Webs of Fate
The Ring of Secret Masters: Rising Through the All Within All
Daggers of the Dying Deep
Bastet's Wealth and Fortune Magick: Prosperity Rituals of the Goddess
The Tide that Speaks
The Scrolls of Petosiris: 13 Rituals from the Feathered Eye
Petosiris and the Living Plague of Osirion
Feline Fire: Bastet's Passion and Love Magick
The Star Altar of Petosiris
Bastet's Whiskers: Supernatural Sensory Magick
The Bastet Grimoire
Feeding the Shadows
The Mouthless Prayer
The Spiral Wound
Becoming the Ibis: Lessons from Petosiris's Mind
The Crimson Coven: Cola Magick for Sweet Dominion
Sacred Cat's Paw
The Soda Zodiac: A Flavor for Every Sign
Covenant of the Crawling Flame
The Ink of Ish'Zur
Frothroot: The Thirst That Ate the World
The Golden Glyphs of Prosperity
The Etherbind Codex
Echoes of the Resistance: Reclaiming the You That Survived
Harnessed Minds: Breaking Free from Mental Control
The Eyes in the Smoke
Rootwake: The Carbon Covenant
Skitter Logic: Unlearning the Fear That Built You

Doctor Who: The World That Froths
Rootwake: The Fizz That Rewrites Flesh
Rootwake: Frothfather of the World
The Holly Pact: Blood Beneath the Mistletoe
The 2nd Mass Principle: Building Unbreakable Tribes
Web of Wits: A Survival Guide to Encounters with Anasi the Spider (Aunt Nancy)
The Hexbreaking Handbook: Effective Spells to Remove Curses
Pop Alchemy: Transform Your Life One Sip at a Time
The Mason Code: Leading in Unleadable Times
Petosiris and the Fifth Chamber of Thoth
The Ether Seed Within
The Parent of Tomorrow
Petosiris's Pyramid of Perpetual Wealth
Unlearn the World
Grimoire of the Hollow Tongue
Zodiac Weeds: Finding Your Strain Through the Stars
Aquarius Rises in the Bank
The Sugar God's Smile
The Skinclock Reversal: Biohacking the Face of Time
Debtburn: How to Obliterate What You Owe Forever
The Ice Cream Oracle: What Your Cone Says About Your Future
Silence Is Sovereignty: The Power of Being Unreadable
The Wind That Whispers Through Stone
Path of the Four Directions
Doctor Who: The Maestro's Symphony of Endings
Oxygen Grail: Breathing to Undo the Clock
Zodiacal Collapse: When Stars Devour Time
Teachings from the Red Sand Silence
Doctor Who: Omega – The Broken Equation
Memory Wipe Your Past: Start Over Like a MiB

Mitochondria Prime: Ignite the Core of Youth
A Nest of Roaches
Grub from the Galaxy: MiB Recipes You'll Never Forget
Whiskers of Power: Bastet's Guide to Inner Sovereignty
The Gift Must Cost Them: Negotiation Through Unequal Exchange
The Worm Guys' Wealth Code: Hustle Like an Alien
Bug Out: The Edgar Method for Ruthless Goal Setting
Weaving Life with Spiderwoman's Pattern
Doctor Who: The Rani's Renaissance
How to Get a Job (If You're a Puppygirl)
Speak Through Others: The Art of Proxy Power
T-Rex Your Trauma: Reclaim the Power of Your Primal Self
The Black Briefcase: How MiB Stay Wealthy in Silence
The Thirst Beyond Reason: Understanding Diabetes Insipidus From the Inside Out
Backwoods Witchcraft for Billionaires: The Pagan Path from Dirt Roads to Gold Roads
The Moonshine Grimoire: Fermented Spells for Abundance
The Nameless Geometry
The Wraith's Mixtape: Spellcasting with Songs of Sorrow
The Gallifreyan Gentleman: Silent Wealth, Sonic Confidence, and the Doctor's Code of Living
Sugar Water Confidence
Dino Totems: Spirit Guides from Earth's First Gods
Pumpkin Sigils & Ritual Smoke
The Hózhó Compass
The Distortus Discipline – Order from Inner Mutation
Witchcraft for the Cold-Blooded Soul
Moonlight Over the Blessingway
Water, Interrupted: When the Body Forgets How to Hold On
Deformed but Divine: Embracing Your Asymmetry
Hexes in the Henhouse: The Farm Witch's Guide to Power

The Reversed Flame: A Grimoire of Inverted Power

Salt, Cells, and Sanity: Reclaiming Balance with Diabetes Insipidus

King of the Broken: Crowning the Flawed Self

Moonlight Scars: Emo Moon Magick and the Art of Lunar Sorrow

Noose Spells: Magick of the Hanging Rope

The Goth Cathedral: Rituals of the Broken and Beautiful

The Cretaceous Codex: Dino Spirits and Fossil Magick

The Turkey Bones Ritual

Nine Lives of Manifestation: Unlocking Bastet's Reality Codes

Chaos Muscles: Building Strength from Twisted Pain

Emo Blood Magick: The Veins of Power

The 3AM Flood: Nighttime Urination, Sleep Loss, and the DI Spiral

The Silence Between the Stars

The Lemon Method: Sour Your Way to Success

Starlit Sovereign

The Rite of Twelve Gates: Walking the Gates of the Duat.

Cornbread and Conjure: Recipes for Riches and Rootwork

The Black Rose Rituals: Emo Love Spells and Obsession Magick

The Eternal Goodbye: Death Magick and Rebirth Rituals

Sinkrot: The Drain That Remembers

The Hybrid Mindset: Thinking Beyond Evolution

Bone Dry: Navigating Dehydration Before It Breaks You

Wreathcraft: Winter Sigils and Yuletide Spells

The Rite of Twelve Mouths

S'mores of the Damned: Haunted Recipes for Halloween Night

Rethink the Drink: A Beverage Survival Guide for DI Warriors

The Shadow Chord: Guitar Magick and Sonic

The Coffin's Lullaby: Sleep Magick and Nightmares as Portals
Ashes of the Will: Rituals for Erasing the Self
The Fracture Rite: Shattering the Magickal Core
Funeral Candles: The Art of Emo Flame Magick
The Black Grimoire: A Blank Ritual for Writing in Absence
Phantom Thirst: A Halloween Survival Guide for Diabetes Insipidus
The Hollow Crown: Emo Royalty and Magick of the Outcast King
Sandpainting for the Soul
Falling Into Balance: Using the Extra Hour to Recalibrate Life
100 Southern Superstitions That Still Work
The DI Child: A Parent's Guide to Raising Hydrated, Happy Kids
The Jungle of Shame: Escaping the Hidden Lab of Doubt
The Witch's Toast: S'mores Spells and Creepy Confections
The Hoodoo Pantry: Spells from the Mason Jar
The Immortal Fortune: Secret Wealth Lessons from Captain Jack Harkness
The Specter's Embrace: Magick for Channeling Ghostly Lovers
Grateful Waters: A Thanksgiving Survival Guide for Diabetes Insipidus
The Seizure Gospel
Harvestbind: Autumn Sigils and Samhain Spells
Doctor Who: The Algorithmic Awakening
Silent Nights, Steady Waters: A Christmas Survival Guide for Diabetes Insipidus
The Extra Hour Effect: How One Hour Can Transform Everything
Blade Between the Breaths
Running with the Mountain Shadows
Echoes of the Failed Experiment – Becoming a Living Legacy

Swamp Witches & River Ghosts: Real Southern Hauntings

Cornbread Prophecies: Magical Recipes from a Southern Table

Doctor Who: The Signal in the Star

Bloomcraft: Spring Sigils and Equinox Enchantments

Vanisher: How to Disappear from the Internet Without Losing Your Life

The Ultimate Christmas Cookie Cookbook

The Unbreakable Parent: How to Mentally Survive Raising Kids in a Broken World

Time Debt: How to Reclaim the Hours You Didn't Know You Lost

One Month, One Million: Unconventional Cash Creation Tactics

Doctor Who: The Cyber Conversion Protocol

Black Friday Frenzy: The Art of Finding Hidden Online Deals

The Grimoire Buried Under the Apple Tree

Digital Couponing Masterclass: Your Step-by-Step Guide to Black Friday Savings

The Fire Inside the Flint

Shadows on the Ceiling: The Emo Guide to Astral Magick

The Bone-Eaters Beneath Us

Black Friday Bundle Blueprint: Creating Irresistible Product Packages for Maximum Sales

Thirteen Nights of Unbinding

Doctor Who: Engines of Influence

Pumpkin Spice Alchemy: Recipes of Fire and Frost

When Raptor Met Rexy: Prehistoric Lessons in Wild Romance

Oblivion's Candle: Burn the Path Behind You

Campfire Curses and Chocolate: A Halloween S'mores Grimoire

The Wallet That Wasn't Mine: Breaking Free from Inherited Scarcity

The Cola Zodiac: What Your Fizz Says About Your Fate

Frostfire Fortune: Unlocking Winter's Hidden Prosperity

Signal Jamming: Detox Your Brain from Info Overload

The Dust of the Forgotten Rite

The Golden Cat Sigils: Drawing Power in Bastet's Name

Mud Magick: The Prosperity of Getting Dirty

Savory Spicefall: Beyond the Pumpkin Pie

Pumpkin Spice Apothecary Kitchen

The Pumpkin Spice Economy: Turning Trends into Billions

The Ember Veil: 13 Nights of Fire Magick

Financial Freeze: When Earning Triggers Panic

The Gingerbread Alchemist: Sweet Recipes with a Twist

Biosynth Power: Programming Yourself from Scratch

Echoes from the Talking Circle

Truffle Alchemy: Fungus of Fortune

Spores of Power: The Truffle Witch's Handbook

Doctor Who: The Tower That Speaks

The Mycelium Veil: Truffle Magick Unbound

Broke But Ashamed: Healing the Shame Wound of Debt

The Evergreen Mind: Growth Through Winter Stillness

The Black Veil Truffle Rite

The Voice Beneath Symbols

Witchlight on the Bayou: Swamp Spells for Sovereignty

I Grew Up Poor and Now I Sabotage My Success

The Lantern of Hollow Souls

Shutdown Survival: A Citizen's Guide to Thriving When Government Stops

When Abundance Feels Like a Threat: Healing the Hidden Fears of Enough

The Scarecrow Grimoire

Owls of the October Veil

Candlewax and Curses: A Halloween Spellbook
Excavating the Inner Fossil – Transforming Fossilized Thoughtforms into Tools of Power
The Yule Witch's Spellbook: Magick for the Holiday Season
Haunted Christmas: Ghost Stories for Winter Nights
The Christmas Survival Guide: Thriving Through the Chaos
The Bone Orchard Rites
Haunted Commerce: The Ghost in the Marketplace
When Money Triggers the Inner Child
Silent Night with the Silence: A Christmas Thriller
The Lightning Crown: Living and Leading Through Seizures
TARDIS Tidings: Festive Stories from the Whoniverse
Autumn Reset: Slowing Down Without Falling Behind
The Trillion Dollar Soul: Rewriting the Currency of Reality
Truffle Eclipse Magick
Micro-Manifestations: Quick Magick That Works
5-Minute Rituals for Busy Witches
The Marshmallow Massacre: Halloween Treats with a Sinister Twist
Blood and Blackberry Thorns
Magickal Mornings: Rituals for a Blessed Christmas Day
Embers of the All-Hallows Fire
The Pumpkin Market Collapse
The Hour You Gained: Transforming Time Into Power
The Chamber Must Be Sealed: Mastering the Power of Controlled Access
The Cursed Manuscript of Petosiris
The Festive Hearth: Creating Holiday Traditions
Darkness Rising: Thriving as Nights Grow Longer
Harvesting Time: Turning the Year's End Into Your New Beginning
Petosiris and the 13th Zodiac Key
Wagewound: When Paychecks Become Identity Prisons

Walls That Watch

The Silent Feast: Rituals of Power in the Longest Night

The Distortus Legacy : Becoming a Deformed King in a Perfect World

The Hollow Masks

The Gratitude Furnace: Forging Gold from Thanks

Feast of Inner Gold: Eating for Energy and Enlightenment

Haunted Commerce: The Season of Spending Spirits

Fear Bonds: How Panic Creates Profit

Black Friday E-Commerce Playbook: Sales Tactics to Skyrocket Your Holiday Revenue

Budgeting for Black Friday: A Holiday Savings Planner

Haunting the Harvest Moon

The Warrior's Water: Emergency Preparedness for People With DI

The First Sip of the Year: A New Year's Survival Guide for Diabetes Insipidus

Doctor Who: The Thirteenth Node

The Unseen Struggle: Mental Health, Anxiety, and Chronic Thirst

The Hearth's Hidden Ledger: Counting Energies as Currency

The Gift Alchemist: Turning Any Offering Into Gold

The Papyrus of the Bound Spirit

The Magick of Leftovers: Transmutation in the Fridge

Frost and Fortune: Christmas Wealthcraft for the Modern Magus

Last-Minute Gifts: Creative Ideas on a Budget

10 Secrets to Surviving Holiday Crowds

The Witch's Dow Jones

The Witches' Graveyard Shift

Pumpkin Sigils: Carving Rites for Midnight Power

The Secret Shopper's Black Friday Guide: How to Get Early Access and VIP Deals

Fever in the Foundation

The Neuralyzer Reset: Reprogram Your Morning Routine

Lightning Lessons of the White Painted Woman

The Enchanted Snowflake

The Magic Sip: Surviving Disney Parks with Diabetes Insipidus

The One Who Draws Through You

Santa's Secrets: A Magical Holiday Planner

Silent Bells, Loud Miracles: Self-Help for the Season of Stillness

The Sugar Spell Codex: Confectionary Magick of Christmas

Autumn Hexcraft: Fallen Leaves, Fallen Barriers

Sleep Like a Fortress: Build a Life Where Insomnia Can't Survive

Nowhere Was Ever Home

Christmas Under the Stars: A Celestial Holiday Guide

Rentproof: How to Never Be Evicted Again

Workless: Escape the 9-5 Without Being Broke

The Gilded Gift: A Wealth Altar for Christmas Morning

The Black Friday Grimoire

The Hollowing: Ceremonies of Spiritual Collapse

Doctor Who: The Nameless Signal

Where the Eagle Hides His Courage

The Dwarf Tyrant's Ascent: Claiming Power in a World of Giants

The Currency of the Dead: Trading with Spectral Bankers

The Icebound Witch: Survival and Magick in the Cold

The Emergency Money Mind: Constant Crisis, Zero Calm

Thirst & Roses: A Valentine's Survival Guide for Diabetes Insipidus

Springing Into Clarity: Mastering the Energy Shift of Daylight Saving

Speed of the Nanotyrant: Agile Strategies for Life's Hunt

The 90-Day Reset: A Science-Backed Guide to Reinvent Yourself Before the New Year

The Coil of Thorns

Timegates Unleashed

Dopamine Fasting 2.0: Rewiring Your Brain in a World of Overstimulation

The Nanotyrannus Mutation: Embracing Your Differentiated Form

Unwritten January: How to Use the Blank Page of the Year to Re-Author Your Life

Feast of the Forgotten Spirits: Ancestor Magick for the Holidays

The Burnout Codex: A System for Thriving Beyond Stress

I Don't Deserve to Have Money

When the King Doesn't See You: The Shadow Predator's Guide

The Reset Ritual :A Guide to Shedding Last Year's Weight—Emotional and Physical—by Spring Cleaning Your Soul

Calendar Alchemy: Learn to Bend Time and Productivity around Your Natural Rhythms

The Mirror Contract: A One-Sentence Agreement with Yourself that Unlocks Real Change

The Nile Formula: Sacred Flow for Millionaire Minds

Forward Momentum: Productivity Rituals for the Lost Hour

Harvest Gold: Wealth Magick of Pumpkin Spice Commerce

The Magick of Christmas Lights: Illuminating Holiday Rituals

Cranberry Crown: Royal Self-Worth through Ritual Meals

Petosiris and the Worms of the Feathered Throne

The Evergreen Equation: Self-Help for Sustained Growth

The Rain Will Wash Us Away: Emo Weather Magick

Snowlight Shadows: Magick Under Frozen Stars

Doctor Who: Merger of Empires

The Light Within the Feast: Magickal Wealth of Yuletide Flame

Momentum Machines: Small Habits Designed to Snowball into Unstoppable Forward Motion

Calm Spells: Magickal Solutions for Anxiety Relief

Santa's Final List: The Naughty Never Leave

The Mystic's Guide to Banishing Worry

The Silence Dividend: Turning Quiet Mornings into Compounding Growth All Year

Charmed Stillness: Rituals to Ease the Mind

Blood Spiral Ascension

The Vanishing Heart Invocation

Crystal Calm: Harnessing Stones for Anxiety

The Nano Tyrant Code: Strength in the Small Predator

The Energy Ledger: Accounting Methods for Vitality, Not Just Money

Snowglobe Mindset: Shake Up Your Thoughts, Settle Into Peace

The Weight of the Feather: Anubis's Codes for Soul Balance

Pocket Peppermint Power: Tiny Rituals for Big Holiday Energy

Shadowkeeper of the Golden Jackal: Anubis's Path to Energetic Protection

The Witch's Breath: Anxiety Relief Through Magickal Breathing

The Tiny Ember: Pocket Motivation for Cold Days

Stocking Sorcery: Mini Spells for Holiday Luck and Prosperity

Warm Hands, Steady Heart: Micro Grounding for Winter Anxiety

The Jackal's Lantern: Guide-Lights for Walking the Dark Path

Anubis's Silent Steps: Rituals for Stealth, Peace & Emotional Quiet

The Fifteenth Doctor: Rewriting the Stars
(Ncuti Gatwa, 2023–2025)

Santa's Shortcut to Success: Micro Habits for a Better New Year

The Midnight Cocoa Manifesto: Comfort Rituals for Hard Nights

Why I Can't Save: Trauma Blocks to Financial Planning

Dino Brain, Mega Goals: Rewire Yourself for Savage Success.

Jurassic Profit: Unearth Your Inner Millionaire Fossil

Scales & Softness: Dating with Dino Heart

Carnotaurus Dreams.

Red Willow Thinking.

Reindeer Resilience: How to Keep Going When You're Exhausted

Candlewick Courage: Lighting Strength in Dark Seasons.

Elf-Mode Focus: Fast Attention Fixes for Busy Seasons

Futureproof Feelings: Emotional Skill-Building for Resilience No Matter What the New Year Brings

The 90-Day Rewire: Transform Your Neural Pathways Before Spring Blooms

Jolly Rich: Christmas Micro-Money Magick for Fast Prosperity.

Gingerbread Gratitude: Mini Practices for a Happier Holiday

Trauma-Spending: When Money Becomes a Drug

Goal Skeletons: Build Minimalist Frameworks for Resolutions That Last

The Snarl Strategy: Growling Back at a World That Silenced You

The Hourglass Reset: Reclaiming What the Clock Took

Yule Claw: Dino Rites of Light in the Darkness

Sacred Circles: Grounding Rituals for Anxious Souls

Clockstopper's Gut: Rebuilding the Core of Time

Winterfire Drive: Harness the Cold Season's Stillness to Ignite Deep Motivation

The 5-Minute Productivity Hack: Small Steps to Big Results

Light Ascending: A Self-Help Guide to Longer Days

Inner Economy: Trade Self-Doubt for Confidence Like a High-Value Currency

Simple Success: Decluttering Your Life for Better Results

The Resilient Mind: Thriving in Tough Times

The 2026 Playbook: Mastering the Year Ahead

The Spring Sleep Solution: Conquering Fatigue After Time Change.

The Hormonal Compass: Navigate Back to Your Youth

Golden Vision: Eating for Your Eye Color with the Power of Ghee

Lionhearted Love: Strength in Relationships

MiB Mindset: Think Like a Cosmic Agent

The Ladder of Small Wins: Climb Out of Stagnation by Stacking Micro-Victories

The Momentum Hour: Gaining More in Less Time.

The Year of You: A Self-Help Blueprint for Unapologetic Self-Ownership

***The Dust That Watches You Back*.**

The Astral Parent

Shadow of the King: The Nanotyrannus Parable

Tiny Tidings of Triumph: Small Wins That Change Your Life

Dwarf Tyrant Rising: When You're the One They Overlook

The Bank Account Mirror: Healing How You See Yourself Through Money

Cretaceous Black

When Love Costs Too Much: Romantic Triggers and Financial Wounds

Dream-Eater's Guide to Wealth

Unzipped Reality: The Jacket That Opens Portals

The Power of No: How to Set Boundaries and Get Rich

Keeper of the Desert Veil: Anubis's Teachings on Illusion & Truth

Redacted Stargates: Stories the SGC Buried

The Clock That Dripped Time

Doctor Who: The Silent Acquisition

Hairline Manifestation: Unlocking Power at the Edge of Thought

Cash-Eater Crickets: How Insects Predict Economic Collapse

Dead Pet Whisperer: Grief Alchemy from the Other Side

The Love Algorithm Is Broken: Hack Romance Before It Hacks You

The Rite of the 8-Limbed Seal

Melt the Moon: A Fire Ritual to Reshape Emotion

Venomous Miracles: Healing Through the Poison Path

Wealth Without Water: The Post-Aquatic Rich Life

The Butterfly Betrayal: When Change Turns on You

The Quiet Upgrade: How Humans Are Secretly Rebuilding Themselves Without Asking Permission

Nobody Taught Us This: The Missing Human Manual for Money, Energy, and Self-Respect

You Were Never Broken: Why Most People Are Reacting Normally to an Unstable World

After the Noise Ends: How Humans Reset When the World Finally Goes Quiet

The Month That Tells the Truth: Why January Reveals What the Rest of the Year Hides

Tremors Party Unleashed: The Ultimate Guide to a Graboids Birthday Bash

Cold Start Human: Rebooting Motivation Without Forcing Momentum

The Year that doesn't start until they say

Love Without Performance: What Connection Looks Like When No One Is Watching

February Is a Mirror: What Love Exposes About You

How We Learned Love Wrong: Uninstalling Cultural Myths About Connection

You Are Not Too Much: Why Needing Love Is Not a Flaw

The Crooked Fence Covenant: Backwoods Boundaries and Witch Wealth

The Day That Keeps Repeating: Why Your Life Feels Stuck—and How to Shift It Gently

Nothing Changes Until Something Softens: Escaping Repetition Without Violence to Yourself

Same Life, Different Ending: How Tiny Choices Rewrite Repetition

The Loop Isn't Punishment: Why You're Being Asked to Learn, Not Suffer

Panic at the Register: Retail Anxiety and Public Shame

The Secret Formula to Becoming an Influencer in 90 Days

The New Rich: How to Retire by 35

Digital Nomad Secrets: How to Travel the World and Make Millions

Burn Your Waiting Room: Escape the Delay Spiral

Strapped for Pleasure: A Complete Guide to Pegging and Strap-On Play

Locked in Desire: A Guide to Chastity Play and Intimate Control

Burrowing into History: Groundhog Day Through the Ages

The Shadow Forecast: The Science of Groundhog Day

Choice Cascades: How One Decision in January Sets Ripples for the Whole Year

The Anti-Anxiety Blueprint: Mastering Fear and Stress for Success

The Ancestral Path of the Jackal Priest

Winterborn Titans: Giants of Ice and Stone
The Extinction Spire
The Emotion That Made Me Millions
Delete Their Voice: Become Unreachable
The Frostbound Mysteries: Mythical Beings of January's Chill
The Roar Within: Unlocking Your Potential
From Burrow to Sky: Groundhog Day Explained
The Boogey Book: Festive Ward-Off Edition
Fooled Ya! The Psychology Behind Great Pranks
April Fools' Alchemy: Transforming Everyday Items into Pranks
Anchor Habits: Root Yourself in Unshakable Routines That Endure Seasonal Change
Emerald Waters: A St. Patrick's Day Survival Guide for Diabetes Insipidus
The Groundhog's Legacy: Myths, Legends, and Facts
Six Weeks of Mystery: The Truth Behind Groundhog Day
The Upgrade Mind: Tech-Like Patches and Updates for Your Mental Operating System
Moon Blood, Star Flesh: Embracing Your Hybrid Nature
Groundhog Lore and Legend: A Complete Guide
You Are the Lie They Can't Kill
Download a Different Reality
The Quiet Advantage: Winning Without Announcing Yourself
A Year of Gratitude: Unlocking Joy
Touch Grass: A Pagan Reset for a Burned-Out Digital World
Cold Start Wealth: Building Financial Power from a Standing Still Point
Astrology Without Fate: Using Cycles Without Surrendering Control
The Future is Remote: Work Less, Earn More, Live Anywhere
Harvest of Silence

The Algorithm Knows Your Name
April Fools' Day for Introverts
Soft Power Systems: Influence That Doesn't Exhaust You
Practical Magick for Real Life: Focus, Intent, and Follow-Through
January Is a Lie: Designing Momentum Without the Calendar
Universal Flow: Managing DI in High-Energy Theme Parks
Electric Allure: Exploring Erotic Electro-Play
The Masked Embrace: Exploring Sensory Deprivation
The Ultimate April Fools' Survival Guide
Splashproof Survival: Waterparks & Wave Pools with DI
Agile Predator, Still King: Crafting Your Speed in a World That Celebrates Size
The Shadow Feast: Groundhog Day's Sinister Side
The Bug's Business Model
Edge of Bliss: Mastering the Art of Tease and Denial
Midnight Alchemy: Rituals for Transformation Between the Old Year and the New
Punxsutawney Bloodlines: A Groundhog Day Horror
The Burrower: Groundhog Day's Darkest Secrets
Buried Alive: A Groundhog Day Horror Story
Blood Moon Markets: The Witch's Guide to Wealth Magick
The Groundhog's Shadow: What It Means for the World
Seasonal Shadows: The Groundhog Day Phenomenon
The Shadow's Curse: A Groundhog Day Horror Tale
Punxsutawney Revealed: A Guide to Groundhog Day
Safari Hydration: Zoo & Wildlife Park Survival for DI
The Foolproof Prank Planner
***Latex Lust: Embracing Fetish Fashion* is a sophisticated**
Whip & Whisper: The Dynamics of Impact Play
The Shadow Burrow Chronicles: Horror Beneath the Ground
Frozen Shadows: A Groundhog Day Thriller
The Groundhog's Revenge: A February Nightmare

Burrow of the Damned
Everyday Enchantment: Magickal Practices for Modern Living
Budget Bliss: The Easy Path to Financial Freedom
Six More Weeks of Terror
The Oxygen Debt
The Ice Veil: Mystical Beasts of January's Shadows
Roots That Remember
Polar Myths: Creatures of the Icy Abyss
The Marginalia Covenant
AI and the Occult: Digital Spirits, Sigils, and Cyber-Witchcraft
Roleplay Realms: Crafting Fantasies and Scenes
The Last Clean River
Lover in the Shadows: A Groundhog Day Tale
Buried Hearts: A Groundhog Day Gothic Romance
Anubis Wept for Petosiris
The Lantern Knows Your Name
Rituals of the Last Shadow
The Bell That Rings for No One
Shadows of Love and Death
The Groundhog's Bride: A Dark Valentine's Tale
Frozen Kisses: A Horror Romance for Groundhog Day
The Creative Spark: Igniting Your Passion Projects
From Cub to King: A Journey of Transformation
Six Weeks to Midnight: A Groundhog Day Romance
Tide of the Unclean
Burrow of Desire: A Groundhog Day Paranormal Romance
The Shadow Magick Almanac: Harnessing Groundhog Day Energies
AI for Emo Influencers: Growing an Online Following Without the Anxiety
AI for the Melancholy Millionaire: Making Money Without Social Interaction

Winter's Grip: A Horror Romance Beneath the Frost
Shadowed Hearts: A Love Buried in Winter's Chill
The Shadow Lover: A Groundhog Day Gothic Love Story
Beneath the Burrow: A Groundhog Day Thriller
The Punxsutawney Conspiracy
The Crimson Pact: Emo Blood Oath Magick
The Shadows of Gallifrey: A Doctor Who Horror Collection
Whispers in the Vortex: Chilling Tales from the TARDIS
AI Ghostwriting for Emo Souls: How to Make Money Writing Without Trying
The Anti-Social Emo's Guide to AI-Powered Freelancing
Emo AI Therapy: Talking to Robots When Humans Suck
Cry & Collect: AI-Powered Passive Income for Emos
The Weeping Angel Chronicles: A Collection of Terror
Dating Without the Mask
The Clockwork Menace: Horror Stories from the Future
Tender Doesn't Mean Weak
Not a Burden, Not a Bonus
Dalek Nightmares: Stories of Ultimate Extermination
The Empty Child's Curse: Tales of Horror and Fear
The TARDIS Ghost Files: Hauntings Across the Universe
Soft Armor, Open Heart
Chosen Gently
Love That Doesn't Rush You
Financial Gaslighting: When You're Made to Feel Crazy About Money.
After the Bees Went Silent
The Soil Knows Your Name
The Quantum Magick Codex: Unlocking the Hidden Laws of Reality
The Gingerbread Golem's Awakening: A Tale of Sweet Revenge

Where Rest Learns Your Name: Six Gentle Bedtime Stories for Minds That Work Differently

Soft Armor for Tender Nights: Six 5-Minute Bedtime Stories for Hearts That Have Been Hurt

Paws of Night, Path of Stars: Six 5-Minute Bedtime Stories Guided by Bastet and Anubis

When the Mind Needs a Lamp: Six 5-Minute Bedtime Stories for Gentle Mental Health Care

Imbolc Roar: Awakening the Dino Flame

The Titan Never Died

Witchflesh Harvest

Become the Thought They Can't Unsee

Golden Threads: The Sensuality of Body Worship

Chains of Desire: Exploring the Beauty of Restraint

Glyphs Written in Organs

Living Below the Line

Palismen Don't Scream—Until They Do

The Boiling Isles Devour the Weak

Hexside Anatomy Lab

Philip Wittebane and the First Body

Money PTSD: When Trauma Hijacks Your Finances

Brother, Bone, and Betrayal

Lipstick Like a Weapon: A Goth Girl's Guide to Emotional Dominance, Boundaries, and Quiet Intimidation

The Scar Is the Portal

Don't Grow—Mutate

Built from Breakdown: The Collapse Code

The Collector's First Lesson

Glyph Failure Syndrome

Philip Wittebane and the Discipline of Lies

The Making of Belos

Flesh Does Not Belong

The Golden Guard Prototypes

Coven Marks as Control Wounds

The Voice Belos Invented

The Boogeyman Within: Shadow Work for Personal Transformation

The Energy Edge: Reclaiming Your Power

Mindful March: A Quick Guide to Intentional Living

Love on Autopilot: Rekindle Your Relationship Instantly

Spring Renewal: Refresh Your Mindset Before the Equinox

Velvet Control: The Subtle Art of Erotic Choking

Erotic Shadows: Playing with Voyeurism and Exhibitionism

The Green Pulse Awakens

Equinox Bones

Immortality Is a Disease

Cold-Blooded Focus

The Invasive Advantage

The Lonely Assassin's Love: A Weeping Angel Romance

Philip Is Still Inside

Become the Signal That Replaces the Noise

When the Soil Says Yes

Shedding What No Longer Protects You

The Shadow Key: Unlocking the Power of Your Dark Self

The Enchanted Chocolate Rituals: Magickal Recipes for Love & Wealth

Love in the Vortex: A Doctor Who Horror Romance

Grimwalker Number Seventeen

The Boy Who Woke Again

Sad Girls Don't Beg: Reclaiming Self-Worth When Melancholy Is Mistaken for Weakness

Raising Pagan Children in a Non-Pagan World

The Pagan Homeschool Exit Strategy

Protecting Childhood While Preparing for Adulthood

Curriculum for the Dead

Too Much for Who? Reclaiming the Power of Intensity

Your Nervous System Is the Algorithm
Memories That Don't Belong to Him
The Golden Guard Template
Time-Locked Hearts: A Gallifreyan Gothic Romance
Ostara's Hatchlings: Fertile Dino Magick
The Dalek's Heart: A Tale of Forbidden Love
The Jackal's Final Game
Where Wild Magic Took My Brother
Where Love Meets Reality
Volume Without Apology
The Mind of Stillness: Petosiris's Hidden Teachings on Power
Doctor Who: The Final Shareholder Meeting
The Archive of Unfinished Lives
AI for Emo Musicians: Automating Your Sad Soundtracks
AI-Generated Emo Art: Selling Melancholy in Digital Form
Ashes Where the Cathedral Slept
The Monarch of Splintered Wings
People-Pleasing Is a Survival Strategy Past Its Expiration Date
Velvet Carnage Covenant
The Intensity Advantage
Attention Is a Finite Resource—You're Overspending It
Emotional Debt Compounds Faster Than Money
The Siege of Thornlit Graves
When the Bone King Wept Black
Comfort Is the Most Expensive Addiction
The AI Gothpreneur: Building a Business Without Any Social Interaction
AI & Tarot: Emo Divination for the Digital Age
Sad AI Aesthetics: Emo Branding & Personal Style
Black Sails Over a Dying Sun
The Crimson Parliament of Wolves
Cathedral of Veins and Thunder
The Orchard of Hanging Saints

The Self-Discovery Path: Find Your True Purpose
You Were Taught to Self-Sabotage Politely
Chrysalis Debt: Reborn into Wealth
Empire of Teeth and Perfume
The Devourer's Bride of Iron Mist
The Dormitory with No Windows
Built Larger Than the Room
The Silence Between Wings
The Manuscript That Grades You
The Librarian Who Refused to Die
Footnotes for a Burning Campus
The Thornblood Accord
The Paranormal Files: True Encounters with Ghosts, Aliens, and the Unexplained
Warfare in the Temple of Shattered Constellations
The Crow's Codex: Unlocking the Secrets of the Black-Winged Messengers
Purring Boundaries: Bastet's Guide to Raising Fierce Children
The Arcane Wealth Formula: Spellcasting for Infinite Abundance
The Celestial Spellbook: Harnessing Planetary Magick for Power and Fortune
Silk Shrouds of the Frostbound Wilds
Windtalker: The Hill Witch's Guide to Whisper Magick
The Doctrine of Psyence: Knowledge Beyond the Veil
The Bone Sovereign's Final War Chant
The Abyssal Altar of Salt and Silver
The Lantern Wilds That Devoured Lovers
The Court of the Sable Scar
Wax & Whispers: The Art of Candle Play
The Billionaire's Blueprint: Unlocking Wealth Through Action

The Cleansing Flow: Unlocking Wellness with Enema Therapy

Seasonal Gratitude: How to Thrive Before Spring

Beyond the Closet Door: Unlocking Your Full Potential by Embracing Fear

The War-Bound Crown

Eternity With Teeth

The Observer Is the Spell: Reality as Psychic Architecture

Mis-Classified Monster: Redefine Yourself

Claws Without Cruelty: The Bastet Discipline Method

Claws Without Cruelty: The Bastet Discipline Method

Temple Mothers: Parenting in the Spirit of the Sacred Cat

The Sixth Extinction You Can Stop

Ticket to the Unseen

The Basement Doesn't Stay Shut

Exhibit of Moving Bones

The Creek That Brings Things Back

No-Exit Hallway

The Tourist Who Knew Their Names

The Limestone Choir

The Room That Remembers Pain

Briar Hollow's Missing Hour

The Gift Shop of Cursed Souvenirs

The Stag in the Ceiling

Two Journals, One Lie

The Museum Eats Its Own Map

The Other Side Leaves Footprints

The Town That Forgets Faces

The Limestone Mouth

The Curator's Ledger of Regrets

The Portrait That Bleeds Tomorrow

The Visitor in Maeve's Voice

The Artifact That Wants to Be Worn

Time is Your Ally: Mastering Productivity with Ease

The Oak Knows Your Name: Forest Witch Wisdom for Wealth

The Rift Exodus

The Fractured Nation

The Coastal Shift

The Lunar Witch's Book of Spells: Moon Magick for Every Phase

Elemental Mastery: The Magick of Fire, Water, Air, and Earth

The Sorcerer's Almanac: Rituals and Spells for Every Season

The Magick of Words: Spells, Chants, and Enchantment for Power

The AI Dating Coach: How to Attract Love in the Digital Age

Boomstick Magick: Fire, Hunting, and the Spell of Sovereignty

Gator Grit: Harnessing the Power of Resilience in Tough Times

The Sky Without Weight

The War Beneath the Soil

The Starborn Code: Awakening the Cosmic Memory in You

The Ritual Alchemist: Transforming Reality Through Sacred Magick

The Stress Detox: 5 Steps to a Calmer Mind

The Object in the Dry Lake

Silence Between the Shelves

The School That Teaches You Backwards

The Witch of Wildcane Ridge: Texas Country Magick for Wealth, Land, and Legacy

Cactus Sigils and Cowgirl Spells: Desert Magick from the Heart of Texas

Rise After the Invasion: Building Confidence in a World That Shattered You

The Silent Pilots

The 5-Minute Gratitude Journal: Transform Your Mindset Daily
Spines of the World
Godseed Protocol
Shattered Bliss: The Art of Erotic Glass Play
Masked Desires: The Thrill of Erotic Costuming
Bound in Bliss: Exploring Mummification Play
Shock and Awe: The Allure of Erotic Fear Play
Drenched Desires: Exploring Water-Based Kinks
Fearless Living: How to Conquer Anxiety and Take Bold Action
The Abyss is Awake
Plankton Crown
Host of the Hollow Current
Marrowlight
Below the Black Tide
The Wishing Vault: Unlocking the Power of Your Desires
The Department That Studies Failure
Midterms Are Held at Night
The Reading Room Without Time
Plagiarism of the Soul
The Choir That Archives Screams
Office Hours for the Unalive
The Index of Forbidden Names
The Phantom's Whisper: A Guide to Ghost Communication
The Campus That Only Exists During Finals
The Librarian of Lost Endings
Students Who Never Took Attendance
The Fellowship of Unpublished Minds
The Exam That Asks Who You Are
Banjo Bones and Spell-Smoke: Sound Rituals of the South
The House That Taught Her Nothing

Twister Wands and Tornado Sigils: Storm Magick of the South Plains

Witchin' in the Kitchen: Texas Pagan Cooking for Magick and Money

The Economy of Bones

Markets of the Dead

The Last Currency Was Blood

Supply Chain of Flesh

The War That Never Ended Inside Us

Hunger City

Beyond the Degree: Becoming Real

The Desert Park Protocol: Diabetes Insipidus Adventures in Hot Climate Parks

Earth School Dropout

The Collapse Harvest

Ride Ready: Six Flags Survival Strategies for Diabetes Insipidus

Galactic Thirst: Surviving Sci-Fi & Movie Theme Worlds with Diabetes Insipidus

Debt in the Dark

The Human Trade

The Haunted Self: Using Shadow Work and the Occult to Heal Your Darkest Fears

The Fairground Flow: Carnival & State Fair Diabetes Insipidus Toolkit

The Debt They Don't Want You to Question

You Are the Curriculum Now

The Coaster Cure: Mental & Physical Balance for Diabetes Insipidus Thrill-Seekers

Blackout Nation

The Price of Staying Alive

Ash Markets

The Quiet Looters

You're Not Lazy, You're Awakening
The Sound of Empty Shelves
The Ration Line
The Anti-Burnout Codex: Thriving Beyond Stress
Sacred Bruises: The Art of Marking in Kink
Scarcity Screams
Spring Waters Rising: An Easter Survival Guide for Diabetes Insipidus
Don't Join the World. Recreate It
The Ceremony Never Needed a Stage
The Bull Witch: Wealth Magick from Rodeo Bloodlines
A world without enough
The Night the Currency Died
The Final Transaction
The Dead Don't Spend
Erotic Alchemy: The Intimacy of Body Painting
AI Magick: Merging Spiritual Energy with Technology for Healing
The Door That Never Closes
Freedom to Hydrate: An Independence Day Survival Guide for Diabetes Insipidus
Strains of Pleasure: A Guide to Pegging and Exploring New Heights
Greenwashed
Caring Waters: A Mother's Day Survival Guide for Diabetes Insipidus
Strong Streams: A Father's Day Survival Guide for Diabetes Insipidus
The Burnout Cure: Reclaiming Energy, Passion, and Joy
The Millionaire Mindset Shift: Think, Act, and Earn Like the Wealthy
Hunger Protocol
The Soda God's Mouth

The Emotional Armor Blueprint: How to Become Mentally Unbreakable

The Last Store Open

The Cost of Breathing

Red Ledger: Everything Must Be Paid

Camps of the Unseen Teachings

When the System Ate Itself

Wealth in the Ash Cycle: Building Power When Systems Collapse

The Boogeyman's Bargain: Turning Your Weaknesses into Strengths

The Boogeyman Effect: How to Control Fear Before It Controls You

Boogeyman Chronicles: Tales from the Dark Corners

When the Boogeyman Whispers: Learning to Trust Your Inner Voice

The Black Market Mindset: Silent Wealth in Loud Chaos

The War-Time Income Engine

Currency of Collapse: How to Profit When Nations Break

The Sip That Sees

The Survival Economy Blueprint

Theme Park Nomad: Traveling Across Multiple Parks with Diabetes Insipidus

Festival Flow: Surviving Music & Light Festivals with Diabetes Insipidus

The Family Flow Handbook: Managing Group Trips with Diabetes Insipidus

Codex Petosirica: Spells of the Pyramid Mind

Silent Trade Networks: Invisible Wealth Systems

Blood of the Scrollmaker: Magick Written in Veins

Adapt or Stay Broke

A Powerful Simple Christmas

The Budget Gift Mastery

The Scarcity Multiplier: Turning Less into Empire

Ocean of Balance: The Cruise Ship Survival Guide for Diabetes Insipidus

Cursed Cabana: A Horror Novella Set by the Sea

Trail of Thirst: The National Park Survival Guide for Diabetes Insipidus

World Flow: The Global Traveler's Survival Guide for Diabetes Insipidus

Subterranean Flow: The Cavern & Cave Exploration Survival Guide for Diabetes Insipidus

Summit Flow: The Hiking & Trail Guide for Diabetes Insipidus

Sunburned Spells: Magick for the Summer Solstice

The Law of Magnetic Influence: How to Make People Instantly Like You

Costume Flow: The Comic Con & Cosplay Survival Guide for Diabetes Insipidus

The Boogeyman Lies: How to Escape the Illusions Fear Creates

Festive Without Financial Regret

The Smart Christmas Wallet

Joy Without Overspending

The Lean Holiday Blueprint

Christmas Without Credit Cards

Rich in Ruins: Wealth Creation After the Fall

The Feather Star Maps

Speak the Sky, Rule the Earth: The Command Rites of Petosiris

The Boogeyman's Playground: How to Thrive in Chaos and Uncertainty

Airport Flow: The Frequent Flyer's Guide for Diabetes Insipidus

Highway Hydration: The Road Trip Survival Guide for Diabetes Insipidus

Sports Flow: Managing Athletic Events with Diabetes Insipidus

The Campfire Flow: Camping & Wilderness Survival with Diabetes Insipidus

Wealth Without Infrastructure

The No-Debt Holiday System

Collapse-Proof Cashflow

Candy Cane Confidence: Peppermint Tricks to Boost Self-Esteem

Island Flow: Tropical Vacation Survival for Diabetes Insipidus

City Flow: Urban Exploration Guide for Diabetes Insipidus Travelers

The Debt That Bleeds at Midnight

Glacier Flow: Cold Weather Adventure Survival with Diabetes Insipidus

The $10 Mindset: Winning When Money Shrinks

Festival Waters: Surviving Music & Art Gatherings with Diabetes Insipidus

Calm in Collapse: Emotional Control When Prices Rise

Celebrate Without Sacrifice

The Holiday Control Plan

The Warpath Within

The Frugal Celebration Code

Moonlight Serenity: Using Lunar Energy to Soothe Anxiety

Give Smart, Not Expensive

The Calm Holiday Budget

Apocalypse Survival 101: A Practical Guide to Thriving in Any Crisis

The Pride Code: Values for a Meaningful Life

You Were Drawn to the Fire for a Reason

The Underground Wealth Protocol

The Thirst Protocol: Surviving When Water Becomes Your Lifeline

The Mouse Plague Protocol
Cabin Fever and Contamination
The Rural Outbreak Manual
Control the Chaos Within
Heatwave Survival Code: Chronic Conditions in Extreme Temperatures
Cold Collapse Protocol: Surviving Freezing Conditions with Limited Mobility
No Power Survival Grid: Living Without Electricity with Medical Needs
Isolation Survival Mind: Thriving Alone with Mental and Physical Conditions
The Eagle and the Serpent
Nutrition for Brain Health: Living with Hydrocephalus
Beautiful Enough to Break the Rules
The Mourning Veil: Emo Grief Magick and Sorrow Spells
The Fragile Body Survival Code
The Survival Blueprint for Fragile Systems
Collapse Survival for the Chronically Vulnerable
The Borderless Army
The Continental Currency
The Discipline of Less
Your Life Without Excess
Weak Flesh, Strong Mind
The Emergency Body Protocol
Death Moth Currency: The Burn Rate of Riches
When the Sky Learned to Bleed Red: 100 Poems for the Vermilion Flycatcher
Frostbite Focus: Staying Sharp in Winter Fatigue
Midnight Salt & Cider
The Cities That Swore First
The Quiet Survivor Method
The Medical Collapse Handbook

The Provinces of Tomorrow

The First Rebellion of Texas

The Resilient Brain: Coping with Hydrocephalus

the Purring Stars of Bastet: Poems from the Moonlit Cat Temple

The Ritual of Becoming Untamed

The Bonefire Within

The Sunbelt Accord

The Northern Silence

Walking the Path of Seven Clans

Fragile in the Fallout

The Androgynous Heart Method

Silk Confidence: Loving Yourself Without Permission

The Mexico City Directive

The Great Language Mandate

The Schools of the New Continent

The Food Scarcity Method: Eating for Survival with Medical Restrictions

Stop Editing Yourself

Mind Over Mattercraft: The Laws of Inner Physics

The Silent Warning System: Listening to Your Body Before It Fails

Shelter Under Strain: Building Safe Spaces with Physical and Mental Conditions

The Moving Body Protocol: Traveling Long Distances While Medically Limited

Compsognathus Through Deep Time

The Hidden Life of Compsognathus

Compsognathus: The Small Dinosaur That Changed Paleontology

Limitless Creativity: How to Unlock Your Genius

The Digital Detox Playbook: Reclaim Your Time and Your Life

The 5AM Mastery: The Ultimate Morning Routine for Success

Emotional Wealth in Empty Times

The Resilient Mind Protocol

Where the Pines Swallow Names

The Continental Census

The Moonlit Architecture of Success

Pagan Mindset Dominion

Flush Fatigue: Restoring Energy Through Colon Care

Small Steps, Giant Results: Lessons from the Compsognathus

The Compsognathus Advantage: Winning Through Agility Instead of Power

Urban Collapse Survival: Navigating Cities with Chronic Conditions

Silent Strength in Loud Struggles

The Collapse Routine: Building Stability When Everything Breaks

Fear Into Fortune

High-Volume Heart

Static Over Velkarrow Isle

The Sensory Survival Guide: Managing Overload in Chaotic Environments

The Breath of Knowing: Psychic Intelligence Training

Ghost Hunting 101: Unlocking the Hidden World of Spirits

The Group Survival Balance: Living with Others While Managing Conditions

Lost Pages of the Doomed

The Recovery Window: Rebuilding Strength After Physical and Mental Crashes

Blackout Body: Surviving Extended Power Failures with Chronic Conditions

ChatGPT Cashflow: How to Automate Your Way to Millions

The Wisdom of the River Cane

Storm Shelter Mindset: Surviving Severe Weather with Medical Challenges

The Pagan Alternative to Grades and Testing

Pagan Parenting for Burned-Out Parents

Balancing Act: Daily Living with Hydrocephalus

The Shunt Whisperer: Caring for Yourself

Yoga and Hydrocephalus: Gentle Practices for Wellness

Pretty Boys Change the World

Mabon Ledger: Harvesting the Hidden Wins

The Haunted Wallet Blueprint

The Pumpkinhead Productivity Method

The October Confidence Ritual

Your Burnout Is a Communication Failure

The Cat Goddess Sleeps in Silver Light: 50 Bastet Poems

Too Intense to Ignore

The South American Question

October Cashflow Harvest

The Fear of Being a Burden: When Help Feels Like Harm

Loved Without Translation: Love Should Not Require Subtitles

The Cozy Reset: Tiny Comfort Rituals for Instant Calm

Emotional Budgeting: Creating a Spending Plan That Soothes, Not Scolds

A Gothmas Carol: Dark Holiday Tales & Traditions

The Quantum Fortune Matrix: Unlocking Infinite Wealth Codes

The Jack-O'-Lantern Kitchen

Fire Circle of the Elders

Raising Little Pumpkins Without the Sugar Meltdown

Feast of the Endlings

The Forgotten Legends of October Nights

The October Budget Survival Guide

The Autumn Imagination Workshop

The Halloween Date Night Guide
Focus When the World Fractures
Incantations of Peace: Spells to Quiet the Mind
The European Panic
The Asian Counterweight
The African Compact
The Arctic Dominion
The War of Frozen Routes
Phantom Discounts II: The Price of the Dead
Phantom Discounts: The Hidden Ledger
Halloween Date Night Recipes for a Romantic Halloween
The Hexmaker's Harvest
The Continental Machine
The Calm Currency
Rituals of Renewal: Pocket Guide to a Balanced Life
Time Mastery: How to Do More in Less Time
The Midnight Harvest Codex
The Silver Pumpkin Grimoire
Nefertiti's Legacy: A Guide to Loving and Caring for Cats with Feline Leukemia
Tyrants of the Starbone Veil
Restoring Energy: Living Fully with Hydrocephalus
Hydrocephalus and Fitness
Imhotep's Guide to Dating and Betrayal: Relationship Lessons from a Man Who Took "It's Complicated" Too Far
Time Management for Hydrocephalus Warriors
The Dalek War Chronicles: The Doctor's Greatest Battles
More are on the way!!!!!!!

www.ingramcontent.com/pod-product-compliance
Lightning Source LLC
LaVergne TN
LVHW030725061126
851857LV00019B/1991

* 9 7 9 8 2 5 6 2 2 3 2 7 4 *